Investigating College Student Misconduct

Investigating College Student Misconduct

Oren R. Griffin

Johns Hopkins University Press • Baltimore

Johns Hopkins University Press
2715 North Charles Street
Baltimore, Maryland 21218-4363
www.press.jhu.edu

Library of Congress Cataloging-in-Publication Data

Names: Griffin, Oren R., 1964– author.
Title: Investigating college student misconduct / Oren R. Griffin.
Description: Baltimore : Johns Hopkins University Press, 2018. |
    Includes bibliographical references and index.
Identifiers: LCCN 2018000283 | ISBN 9781421426372 (pbk. : alk. paper) |
    ISBN 9781421426389 (electronic) | ISBN 1421426374 (pbk. : alk. paper) |
    ISBN 1421426382 (electronic)
Subjects: LCSH: College discipline. | College students—Legal status, laws, etc. |
    Education and crime. | Criminal investigation.
Classification: LCC LB2344 .G75 2018 | DDC 371.7/82—dc23
    LC record available at https://lccn.loc.gov/2018000283

A catalog record for this book is available from the British Library.

*Special discounts are available for bulk purchases of this book. For more information,
please contact Special Sales at 410-516-6936 or specialsales@press.jhu.edu.*

Johns Hopkins University Press uses environmentally friendly book materials,
including recycled text paper that is composed of at least 30 percent post-
consumer waste, whenever possible.

To my wife, Theresa, and to our children, Andrew and Matthew

Contents

Foreword

After almost three decades of dedicating my life to higher education law and policy, my greatest satisfaction still comes in working with rare colleagues like Oren Griffin. We first met many years ago as he began collecting valuable experience as a practicing lawyer in the field of higher education, working as a professor and associate dean, and building his scholarly profile with terminal degrees in law *and* higher education (still a rare combination). These days although we work at separate institutions we present and speak together regularly; notably at the annual Stetson National Conference on Law and Higher Education (which I chair) where we have run a successful "Boot Camp" on higher education law and policy for many years now. Oren is a tremendous colleague—and I have been fortunate to work with him as his extraordinary career has matured—but he is more than a colleague. He is a trusted friend whom I turn to when I am confused or simply need to see things in a wider perspective. Do you remember the kind of teacher who always uplifted you and clarified things? I urge you to let Oren, a teacher of interdisciplinary teachers, guide you with his book through what might seem to be an otherwise inaccessible topic.

I remember clearly when Oren first approached me with the protean yet prescient ideas for this book. He was anticipating what suddenly is now ubiquitous in higher education—the rise of *investigation culture*. Can you recall the times before the Penn State scandal and its Freeh Report, before the April 2011 Dear Colleague Letter launching a thousand investigations under Title IX, before the meltdown at Michigan State University? It is now clear that the Duke lacrosse controversy many years back was a signal of things to come regarding investigations related to *students*, and that recent situations involving registered student organizations like the one at Oklahoma implicating a fraternity may become more common. As higher education has increasingly found itself at the center of controversies there has been a concomitant rise in calls for *accountability*, with a notable increase in emphasis on matters regarding and impacting students. The rise of investigation culture in higher education is a direct result of demands for both internal and external accountability—on campus, in the courts, and in the court of public opinion. Upon examination one thing has become clear: there has been a lack of strong *scholarship* specifically tuned to investigations in higher education. This book is a critical resource written by a professor who can go to court, filling a gap in the literature in a time of need.

Investigations in higher education come in many forms and can serve all sorts of purposes. The book carefully walks the reader through the multidimensionality of investigations: investigations might serve to evaluate institutional performance, prepare for litigation, parallel a government investigation, or help to frame public narratives around a contentious issue or set of issues, *inter alia*. Investigations share many common characteristics but also diverge greatly in scope, purpose, duration, breadth, accessibility, etc. The book is a resource for anyone who wants to learn more about investigations in higher education, and it will become a classroom resource for teachers with pupils who seek to become investigators or interact with investigations on campus. In addition, this book will be especially helpful for individuals currently performing or supervising investigations, such as Title IX administrators, discipline officers, human resources officers, equal opportunity administrators, housing directors, general counsel, outside counsel, etc.

It's a little hard to imagine reading a book on investigations in one sitting. However, Oren brings his down-to-earth, breezy writing style to bear perfectly in this work. Predictably, this book explains key concepts and operational details of investigations in a way that legally and nonlegally trained individuals can readily grasp. The years and years of interdisciplinary experience Oren has accumulated makes reading this book, shall I say, *easy* (perhaps it's his roots in New Orleans?). Keep in mind as you travel through this book that your author does not just write *about* investigations—he *performs* them as a recognized go-to expert in the field. He has also been on the front lines of litigation, and not in the distant past. The book is the product of an experienced, battle-hardened *current* expert. Do not expect armchair musings in this book from a professor *imagining* the realities of investigations, or a stale recitation of experiences past the expiration date.

The book also brings your author's special feel for higher education, clearly written by someone who is sensitive to today's realities in higher education. This book is finely tuned to higher education culture and is responsive to trends in multiculturalism, intersectionality, and the impacts—positive and negative— of an increasingly juridical culture in higher education. Oren and I are both disciples of the now-retired all-time-great professor Parker Young, who can be credited with starting the interdisciplinary law and policy movement decades ago in Georgia. I heard Professor Young once express concerns about the limits of the law in higher education—in his own far superior way. This book is Parker-esque in that way; it is not a patronizing tome written by a lawyer who believes he has all the answers, or a gushing invitation to turn our campuses into quasi-courts of law. The book instead reflects its author's wisdom—quietly emphasizing the power of forbearance and the virtue of temperance. Oren will show you both how to use the law and how best *not* to use it. We have often talked about his grandfather who taught Oren how to use every tool just the right way. This book is a monument to craftsmanship and the fine art of using blunt instruments like law only when needed. It also reflects his grandfather's wisdom—taught to Oren as a young boy—in getting the job done correctly, when it needs to be done.

As I am writing this the season is changing from winter to spring, the weather outside as disruptive as the current climate in higher education. The business of higher education I have known for so long faces gale force winds of accountability. *Printemps* is both a dangerous and regenerative time: Oren's tour of investigation culture will help you, the reader, encounter the sometimes bedeviling challenges of investigations and anticipate the power of positive transformation embedded in every well-run investigation. I assure you, you will never look at investigations the same way. May you enjoy getting to know the author and his subject as much as I have.

Peter F. Lake
Professor of Law, Charles A. Dana Chair,
and Director for the Center for Excellence in Higher
Education Law and Policy
Stetson University College of Law, Gulfport, Florida

Preface

As Student Government Association president during my junior year of college at Southern University in New Orleans, I was asked by the chancellor, Dr. Emmitt Bashful, to attend a funeral with him for a student who had died in a tragic car accident. Nothing dramatic happened at the funeral, and Dr. Bashful, a no-nonsense administrator and professor of political science, did not make any rousing comments at the ceremony about the student or his unfortunate death. However, his decision to be there, supporting the family suffering their loss, has stuck with me for years. The reality was that we lost a student, and the loss of that student resonated with Dr. Bashful and, later, with me. It was important for us to be there.

All too frequently, colleges and universities lose students because of tragic fatalities, but sometimes the loss is related to academic or behavioral misconduct within our educational programs and campus activities. Students can be suspended, expelled, or dismissed from campus for a period of time. When these mishaps occur it is imperative that we investigate what went wrong and learn from these misadventures to minimize any potential recurrence. Whether I have served in the capacity as a lawyer, faculty member, or an academic administrator, this has always been a noble goal of the investigation. However, regardless of strategy or tactics used to conduct an investigation of student misconduct, I have remained convinced that those of us who have anchored our careers in higher education must maintain a vivid sense of how important it is to be there for "our students." In many ways, this book is about managing the risks and potential legal liability that can flow from the often unpredictable work of student affairs. But from another stand-point, this book recognizes that students will make troublesome decisions or just find themselves in harm's way, and administrators and faculty members need to be with students during times of triumph and disaster.

I have long held an appreciation for the challenges that confront the higher education community. Bolstered by my doctoral studies at the University of Iowa and with the aid of Lelia B. Helms, Alan B. Henkin, and Robert E. Engel, I have sought to merge my respect for the rule of law with my interest in complex organizations. As a practitioner representing public and private sector employers, which have included colleges and universities, I have witnessed firsthand that the internal investigation process has remained an intriguing tactical option for decision-makers. I will always be grateful for the lessons learned from Brent Wilson, a highly skilled lawyer and tremendous mentor during my tenure with the Elarbee Thompson firm in Georgia, as well as my time working with Tom Hustoles and Len Givens at the Miller Canfield firm in Michigan. The practice of law has been a tremendous gateway for me, one that is hard to overstate.

As for this book, it has been supported by input from several friends and colleagues including John D. Marshall, Jr., Michael S. Dean, Stephana Colbert, John Somervill, Joseph Marion, Thomas A. Butcher, Johnny Parker, Dorothea Beane, and John E. Hart. I would also like to extend my thanks to Michael A. Olivas and the Institute for Higher Education Law & Governance at the University of Houston Law Center for the encouragement provided regarding this project. Moreover, it is important to mention that writing this book might not have been possible without the support provided by the Mercer University School of Law, especially the assistance provided by law librarians John Perkins and James Walsh. Also, I owe a huge debt of gratitude to my friend Peter F. Lake and our colleagues at the Stetson University College of Law, Center for Excellence in Higher Education Law and Policy. For several years, I have had the pleasure to participate in Stetson's National Conference on Law and Higher Education and this book has been advanced by that community of scholars and higher education professionals.

In addition, the wonderful collection of professionals at Johns Hopkins University Press deserve my thanks for the long hours and effort they devoted to bringing the book through each phase of production.

Finally, I want to thank my wife, Theresa, and our two sons, Matthew and Andrew, for the love and support we share daily. I could not have done this without them.

Investigating College Student Misconduct

Introduction

An internal investigation is a self-imposed inquiry intended to provide answers. Whether in business, government service, or on a college campus, conflict does arise and things can go terribly wrong. In the context of disputes involving students at colleges and universities, internal investigations routinely examine incidents that may violate the institution's code of conduct, examination procedure, faculty protocol set out in course syllabi, student organization rules, or even civil or criminal law. While objectives of an investigation include clarification of the allegations and students involved, the identification of important facts, and likely policy violations, if any, an internal investigation should not be a sophisticated finger-pointing exercise.

Student activity permeates the college environment, but the resolution of student misconduct matters often is led by student affairs administrators. Student affairs administration is unique to higher education and goes beyond ensuring that students are satisfied with their experience at the university or college, and whether they would recommend the institution to others. Student affairs work is carefully aligned with the academic mission and business operations of higher education institutions. This division within the institution's organizational structure recognizes that the student's successful completion of a degree program will involve developmental experiences inside and outside the classroom. More specifically, for college or university students who find themselves embroiled in controversy or acts of misconduct, the work of the student affairs professional often involves administering the disciplinary process that will adjudicate and, one hopes, productively resolve student misconduct allegations.

However, student services personnel are not law enforcement officers and should not be viewed as student punishment arbitrators. For many years, scholars, academic administrators, and legal counsel have discussed at length the viability of the in loco parentis doctrine but, at best, it represents a historical model for the relationship between students and institution. It is true that student affairs administrators must observe and be vigilant in recognizing a student's due process rights, especially when a student may face expulsion or suspension for academic or behavioral misconduct. Nonetheless, it is "the paramount duty and responsibility of educational authorities to maintain an atmosphere on campus which is conducive to the educational function."[1]

This "paramount responsibility" can be satisfied by equitable disciplinary hearings, where students accused of misconduct are given notice and an opportunity to respond to any misconduct charges, as well as the thoughtful, well-reasoned investigation that precedes disciplinary action. The American judicial system stands as a model for resolving disputes, and student disciplinary hearings borrow from the law and our nation's judicial system in the interest of reaching fair and equitable outcomes for students. For controversies and disputes involving students at community colleges, four-year colleges, or universities, the results of an efficient, comprehensive investigation performed within the institution by skilled impartial investigators can resolve conflict and grievances. Further, an internal investigation may uncover valuable information that can improve decision-making regarding academic or behavioral misconduct or do away with the need for more formal student disciplinary proceedings.

Throughout this book, various aspects of the internal investigation and the legal rights of students are reviewed relative to student misconduct at colleges and universities. Since the 1960s challenges for student affairs administrators have become more voluminous and complex. Certainly, institutions of higher education have for many years sought to insulate themselves from legal liability that might flow from student misconduct matters. Herein the focus centers on providing members of the college and university community a resource for conducting the student misconduct internal investigation.

The Aspiration for Higher Education

We live in a competitive world where students, supported by their parents and loved ones, are searching for a path to prosperity and personal achievement. For American families striving to advance the next generation, the reliable way forward traditionally has involved the pursuit of a college education. An earned degree beyond high school and on to graduate and professional schools is a conventional, honorable, and trusted path for many. Whether the journey begins at the community college level, a public regional university, or a small private college, the objective is generally the same—to prepare oneself for a rewarding future by attaining a postsecondary education.

In addition to the worries about the financial expense and demands that come with the hours and hours of academic study required to earn a college degree from an accredited institution of higher education, there are concerns with outcomes. Has the student selected the right degree program? Will the student's grade point average or class rank be high enough to merit an internship or other career-launching opportunities? What will the job market yield after graduation? And on a more personal level, will the connection between college life and individual satisfaction be worth the investment? College students are not robots, artificial beings, or superheroes with the skills required to join the Avengers. Students are just people with human imperfections, but they aspire to a better life.

As the pursuit for advanced degrees at colleges and universities has intensified and the costs for would-be graduates has continued to escalate, the demands and expectations from students, parents, financial donors, and the general public have soared. Students are increasingly portrayed as consumers while faculty and administrators at institutions of higher education are viewed as service providers. But the pursuit of the postsecondary degree for college students is not simply a bundle of services nor is it confined to the classroom, library, or residence halls. *For students, college and university life provides an opportunity to experience growth and make choices—some mature ones and some poor ones.*

When students make poor choices and are called upon to account for them, student affairs personnel, faculty, and other campus administrators are asked to manage and resolve the outcome of such mishaps. Where the resolution of student misadventures involves potential disciplinary action, senior executives and campus administrators are not immune from allegations of wrongdoing. Unjust student disciplinary decisions can have consequences for the institution. Students and their advocates may opt to become plaintiffs, even frustrated faculty or staff personnel who believe that they have been done a disservice by the institution and key decision-makers may choose to take action. Thus, the internal investigation represents a good faith effort to discover and examine relevant facts regarding misconduct allegations and craft a reasonable responsive course of action.

The internal investigation of student misconduct and the fruits of the investigation process offer protection to the institution, the administration, and students against erroneous disciplinary action that can place a student's future in jeopardy or put an avoidable stain on a student's academic record.[2] While not every incident regarding student misconduct requires an internal investigation, colleges and universities are increasingly propelled into student affairs disputes that raise complex legal questions with serious consequences. Student disputes in some cases can result in media attention that can impact the institution or public relations in general. Done effectively, an internal investigation can be a constructive preemptive method that determines the substance of allegations, persons involved and the degree of their involvement, potential legal liability, and options of mitigating loss or harm. However, implemented without adequate attention to scope, purpose, and planning, an internal investigation may result in a missed opportunity for dispute resolution.

The academic experience provides students with a tremendous opportunity for intellectual growth and development. The American collegiate journey transpires within an institutional and social framework that will inundate students with choices and decisions. That "institutional framework" can be presented in various settings including the community college campus, undergraduate college, or the research university with numerous graduate and professional programs, all offering a wide range of degrees as well as diversified social and professional interaction. For students transitioning directly from high school, college life represents new-found freedom, completely devoid of the customary oversight provided by parents or teachers or the accountability relationships developed in secondary school, churches, or in hometown neighborhoods. For other students, for example those returning to postsecondary education after interrupting their studies to care for family members, pursue alternate careers in the workforce, or serve in the military, college represents a path to new opportunities. Regardless of their background, most students will find that the new demands accompanying college life will spark personal introspection or soul-searching regarding the path of their future. Put succinctly, the pursuit of a college education can and should be a glorious endeavor, and every effort should be made to ensure that a student's matriculation proceeds without interruption.

The Rise of the Internal Investigation

Despite the promise offered by higher education, college students can and often do make poor choices from time to time. When student choices result in academic or behavioral misconduct, the institution must be prepared to respond with remediation and fairness in mind. An institution's capacity to independently investigate student misconduct incidents can be a tremendous asset, enhancing an administrator's ability to make informed decisions in a timely manner. This advantage provided by internal investigations to identify and address problems before substantial harm can result was initially recognized by the corporate sector. In the 1960s and 1970s, federal agencies such as the Securities and Exchange Commission (SEC) began to pursue enforcement of federal securities laws for civil and criminal misconduct by officers, directors, and employees.[3] As the consequences grew critical for corporations, many began to initiate internal investigations to avoid potential regulatory and legal problems. For colleges and universities, whether the possible legal problems stem from an NCAA (National Collegiate Athletic Association) violation for misconduct by a student-athlete or a sexual assault allegation under Title IX, the reality is that student misconduct matters must be resolved with great care for the interests of the student and the institution. The internal investigation creates this opportunity.

The impact that student misconduct can have on a campus community can range from the mundane or ordinary disturbance to events that are disruptive. For instance, in March 2015 members of a fraternity at the University of Oklahoma were captured on videotape singing a racist and offensive chant that was later seen across the world through social media and countless news outlets. The incident triggered campus protest and public outrage.[4] The University of Oklahoma president David Boren launched an immediate investigation and took action, banning the fraternity chapter from campus in the wake of the incident. Also, the fraternity's national office closed the chapter and suspended its members shortly after the video was disclosed. For the University of Oklahoma community, what could have been an ordinary social outing for a student organization became a focal point for nationwide concern. Higher education administrators frequently—and often without notice—become the point-persons for colleges and universities to determine, clarify, and confirm "what happened" when alleged acts of student misconduct occur.

When incidents regarding academics or behavior directly or indirectly interrupt the college student's matriculation and his or her life, careful information collection and analysis is necessary to guide administrative action. By gathering evidence and interviewing witnesses at the earliest possible opportunity, the campus personnel performing the internal investigation can allow administrators to consider swift action. Moreover, a prompt inquiry may prevent an incident from growing in complexity or the recurrence of harm. The investigation of student misconduct incidents, however, should not be viewed as a mere administrative exercise but rather as an opportunity to discover what student choices or decisions may have led to behavior or conduct that requires an intervention. Possible mediation strategies or corrective action can range from informal counseling to full-blown disciplinary measures.

The student development literature has long provided valuable insight regarding the college experience and the likely circumstances that can ignite counterproductive and in some situations unpredictable student behavior.[5] Although it may be convenient to categorize student misconduct as immaturity, mischief, a rules violation, or something akin to criminal behavior, student development theory offers various conceptual viewpoints beyond simple disciplinary labels to explain student behavior and perhaps guide corrective action to hold students accountable for their misdeeds. For administrators charged with investigating student misconduct and assessing compliance failures, rules violations, or other legal transgressions, lessons learned from the clinical and social science arena as well as the commonsense realities that accompany the student experience can be important considerations.

However, maintaining a broad spectrum on student misconduct matters can be challenging. Internal investigations in higher education borrow heavily from the approach used by attorneys and executives in the corporate, for-profit, and criminal justice settings which values *precision* and *focus* but can have a narrow perspective where outcomes are measured in quantitative terms such as the impact of student misconduct on tuition revenue, enrollment, recruiting, or campus crime statistics monitored pursuant to the Clery Act. Hence, colleges and universities that are substantially driven by enrollment may be placed in greater jeopardy by egregious student misconduct incidents. The effect a student misconduct matter has on an institution of higher education may also be influenced by organizational form. The establishment of public colleges and universities across the country is largely linked to state constitutional or legislative action (action by politicians, lawmakers, or the public). On the other hand, private colleges and universities find their origin and structural beginnings traced to the assembly and formation of private associations or religious entities that entered contractual relationships and created institutions as private nonprofit corporations. These groups may respond differently to various types of student misconduct. In both instances, whether through government regulation or private action by various stakeholders, the internal investigation is a sound risk-avoidance strategy. Besides institutional form, the application of proven investigation strategies and tactics from the corporate context to student misconduct investigations is influenced by a desire to bring legitimacy to the investigation process.

Going forward, as colleges and universities strive to discover innovative methods to solve student affairs problems and minimize an institution's exposure to legal liability, dependence on internal investigations will continue to rise. Whether the institution is public or private, when confronted with a student misconduct matter the general objective is the same: the general welfare of all students and the safeguarding of the institution's mission. This does not minimize the importance of avoiding legal liability, especially when a student misconduct incident can lead to substantial campus unrest, but instead emphasizes that before disciplinary action can be imposed or the inquiry conducted, the aim of the student misconduct investigation should be well defined to protect our students and campus community.

Understanding the Aim of Student Misconduct Investigations

Students can find themselves embroiled in matters demanding that campus officials conduct internal investigations for allegations on a range of subjects. The student misconduct investigation is guided by a rational framework centered on prevention, process, and restoration. An outline of a likely framework from which internal investigation strategies and tactics emanate is provided in table 1.

A misconduct investigation is typically focused on determining whether the student's alleged behavior or problematic conduct has resulted in a violation of established campus policies (e.g., those detailed in the student handbook, code of conduct, etc.) or has placed the student or members of the campus community at risk for harm, injury, or liability. While the nature of the student misconduct (e.g., sexual assault, offensive speech, or plagiarism/cheating) frequently receives much of the attention, an

TABLE 1. *The Framework for Internal Investigation Decision-Making*

Preventive Law
  Commence the investigation
  Avoid premature action
  Recognize triggering events and limitations of standard systems
  Demonstrate accountability

Investigation Process
  Authorize goals and scope of investigation
  Decide who conducts the investigation
  Determine if special expertise is required
  Gather facts and information
  Conduct interviews and manage documents while preserving privileges and other protections

Remedial/Restorative Institutional Response
  Manage outcomes
  Report investigation results
  Disclose findings

----

underlying goal of the student misconduct investigation is often in the background: *prevention*. The decision to commence an internal investigation in any organization is a recognition that an entity's standard operating systems are unable to identify and manage the alleged misconduct, thus the internal investigation is in some ways a supplemental preventive step. Likewise, there are other reasons that might trigger the desire for an institutionally sponsored internal investigation—such as the need to demonstrate a legitimate level of accountability to various stakeholders, including parents, alumni, governmental officials, and the general public, to ensure that the student community has not become a haven for mayhem or chaos. Put another way, the investigation is tasked with providing relevant information to avoid premature or poor decision-making in the wake of the alleged misconduct.

Furthermore, the internal investigation is a guided *process* that has goals and objectives seeking to separate fact from fiction, identify the relevant regulations, rules, or laws that are implicated by the alleged conduct, and provide student affairs decision-makers with information and documents untainted by conjecture or speculation. Hence, a primary value of the investigative effort will center on the detection of material facts that substantiate a student's alleged misconduct.[6]

And finally, through the investigation process, the hope should be to achieve a measure of *restoration* for the students involved or affected by any misconduct in a manner consistent with the policies, procedures, and practices of the college or university. This restorative goal will be advanced by sharing the results of the investigation in a manner that demonstrates that the institution is transparent, forthcoming, and prepared to take responsibility for its actions. More importantly, by placing a value on restoring students, not simply discovering misconduct, the university may gain credibility among numerous stakeholders.

Consider the 2006 incident involving members of the Duke University men's lacrosse team, who were accused of sexually assaulting a female stripper at an off-campus location where a party was held and the alleged criminal behavior occurred.[7] While the emotionally charged public outcry and protest initially called for prosecuting the student-athletes charged with sexual assault, a detailed investigation of the evidence failed to support claims by local prosecutors that the students were guilty of a crime. Unfortunately, the absence of reliable evidence was only discovered and verified after months of protest and social unrest surrounding the incident, which garnered national attention. In this case, an early, careful investigation of the relevant facts would have revealed no support for the sexual assault allegation and might have calmed the heated protest that placed students and the community at odds. However, the students involved were placed in harm's way long before facing criminal misconduct charges. The choices and decisions made to "hire a stripper" and the presence of alcohol in the situation, while perhaps not strictly illegal, had consequences. But could these consequences have been avoided? More importantly, how can administrators at colleges and universities learn from this and other similar incidents to help students steer clear of such controversy in the future?

An internal investigation is a problem-solving effort—providing administrators with information to prompt action in response to student misconduct as well as offering insight that might be utilized to prevent future incidents. The Duke lacrosse matter and others involving student off-campus ventures are extraordinarily challenging, but an internal investigation allows administrators to candidly examine the performance of an institution's risk-management, safety, and other deterrents used to minimize student misconduct. An investigation can pursue a wide or narrow range of concerns. What preventive measures are in place to monitor the off-campus activities of student groups? What interaction do student groups have, or fail to have, with faculty advisors, coaches, and other support personnel regarding various activities that "open the door" to troubling incidents? Have students been exposed to counseling, workshop training, or mentoring programs regarding the risky behavior? With this type of information, the internal investigation should move along a well-defined trajectory. First, it should be based upon a framework with a defined purpose—to restore order within the curricular and extracurricular systems within the institution. Next, the internal investigation should resist mundane exploration and instead focus on problem-solving. Finally, the value-added internal investigation must lead to improved decision-making (see figure 1).

Because an investigation can be triggered by complex circumstances and reasons that may not be discovered through traditional fact finding, it is critical that the scope of an internal investigation be established and that the goals of the internal investigation be appropriately tailored and not overbroad.[8] The importance of understanding what are and what are not the goals of an investigation cannot be overstated. An internal investigation could be better titled as a "learning

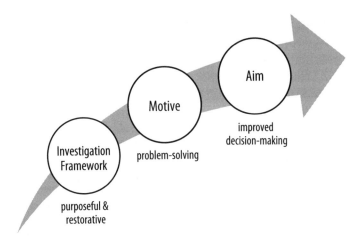

Figure 1. Trajectory of the Internal Investigation

investigation" wherein much will be discovered. Because colleges and universities are loosely coupled systems in terms of the organizational structure, staff members and administrators at every level can be surprised to learn that academic and student affairs policies are implemented each day across their campuses with some degree of variance.[9] Perhaps every internal investigation should be expected to discover some nuances or slippage between institutional policy and campus operations. The critical task is not to become consumed by the secondary topics or volume of information produced by the investigation, but to aim for reaching decisions that are justified and in the best interest of students. This is where training of investigators can be crucial.

The Legal Defense and Institutional Policy

The investigation is intended to identify witnesses, take statements, and determine the sequence of the events regarding an alleged student misconduct incident. However, an over-arching demand that cannot be ignored by student affairs and academic officials includes compliance with state and federal law.[10] In recent years, the emphasis placed on legal compliance has become a critical concern for on-campus administrators as well as the institution's legal counsel and others involved in preparing colleges and universities to mount a legal defense to matters related to student misconduct.

For persons authorized to direct internal investigations, an underlying concern will be determining what reporting or compliance obligations flow from the investigation. For those departments or units firmly within the scope of an investigation that have a substantial number of personnel or operational functions, identifying the breadth of the compliance demands will be a vital undertaking. Given the current and likely future climate regarding legal compliance, institutions of higher education are compelled to rely on the student disciplinary systems while preparing for the worst. When applicable, the results of the internal investigation should aid those responsible for legal compliance and for mounting an institution's legal defense by:

- identifying and categorizing students and other personnel critical to the investigation;
- verifying campus regulations, policies, standards, and legal violations that may be implicated by the alleged misconduct;
- collecting statements, documents, evidence, or other sources of information that may lead to verifiable facts to determine what wrongdoing has occurred and which parties are responsible;
- analyzing information and data collected that provides a sequencing of pertinent events identifying acts of misconduct and responsible individuals.

A routine component of legal compliance, as well as preparation in anticipation of litigation, includes the production of documents and related evidence ordinarily generated by the department or units under investigation. Hence academic departments and student affairs units such as student activities, housing and residence life, the student union, student health center, career services and placement, fraternity and sorority life, counseling and wellness, multicultural affairs, and others within the institution implicated in a student misconduct investigation should be able to demonstrate that the day-to-day transactions or routine activities comply with federal and state law, best practice, and the relevant guidance available.

Investigations can and often do range from the exploration of modest incidents of student conflict to the painstaking examination of matters involving assault, personal injury, or even wrongful death. Regardless of the complexity of the investigation or the subject of the wrongdoing, the investigation seeks to discover relevant facts and clarify the events surrounding the alleged student misconduct. By identifying what information and/or witnesses are consistent and reliable, the internal investigation provides the university or college with the opportunity to make credibility determinations that are vital in response to compliance and legal challenges.

Litigation and Internal Investigations

An institution's administrative leadership is expected to navigate the legal landscape and avoid liability that may flow from lawsuits filed against a college or university and the increasing regulatory demands imposed by governmental agencies. While there may have been a time when students or parents were reluctant to sue a university or college in state or federal court, that era is part of American history. Governmental agencies, public sector employers, and private corporations frequently find themselves in legal disputes as defendants, and they need to rely on the skills and good judgment of their employees and workforce to ensure that the organization remains in a strong position to mount a defense to potential legal challenges. Colleges and universities are no different. Student affairs personnel and academic administrators must have an understanding of the litigation process and what significance the investigation process may have on a civil lawsuit brought against a college or university.

Every lawsuit has a beginning. Conflict is unavoidable regardless of the setting. Whether the matter involves a dispute among neighbors or a routine traffic accident, the inability to resolve conflict can be disruptive and counterproductive. Consider this example:

> Following an on-campus talent show and concert sponsored by the Student Government Association, students get into a shoving match while exiting the auditorium that leads to a brawl between two students in the on-campus parking lot. Both students deny being the aggressor and say they were acting in self-defense. One of them has been disciplined in the past for fighting and other acts of misconduct while the other has no record of misbehavior. A concerted effort to determine the facts surrounding this incident and what involvement each student had in the mishap will obviously be important. However, viewing the facts objectively will also be vital to the investigation to ensure fairness and justify any disciplinary action.

For conflict that impacts the life of students, the investigation process can and should be embraced as an effort that allows the institutional decision-makers to assess what has happened and identify what can be done to resolve the conflict. Viewed as preemptive action, the investigation process has the potential to result in dispute resolution, obviating the need for parties to pursue litigation in state or federal court. In the absence of this preemptive measure, campus administrators are often left to engage the student disciplinary process (i.e., notice, hearing, appeal option, final decision) with limited information. In the event the institution's action does result in a lawsuit, each step taken by university personnel will be scrutinized and litigated.

The litigation process starts with a *complaint* filed by the plaintiff identifying the court's power and authority for presiding over the lawsuit and the parties (plaintiffs and defendants) to the litigation. Also, the complaint sets forth the factual allegations that support the lawsuit as well as the claims and remedies sought by the plaintiff. Once served with the complaint, the defendant is obligated to provide a responsive pleading known as an *answer* wherein the defendant may admit, deny, or indicate that he has insufficient information to admit or deny allegations raised in the complaint. In cases where the college or university is confronted with a lawsuit, drafting the answer will be easier if the university can rely on the results of a thoroughly prepared internal investigation regarding events that produced the lawsuit. Drafting the complaint and the answer, also referred to as the *pleading phase* of litigation, can be a technical process because the failure to properly assert claims and defenses accurately can lead to *amended complaints* that include more claims or challenges that seek to dispose of a lawsuit by a *motion to dismiss*. An internal investigation provides the institution with particular insight into potential liability facing the institution and what defenses may, or may not, be effective in litigation.

Likewise, where an internal investigation reveals that the institution has legitimate exposure to legal claims and/or potential liability, the university decision-makers can rely on the available information to take remedial action, weigh the threat or harm posed to the institution and students, and for purposes related to anticipated litigation, assess *settlement options*. Yes, settlement, or alternative dispute resolution methods, should remain an option as legal claims proceed through the litigation process. The perspective gained from conducting an internal investigation gives the college or university some vision regarding the strength of evidence that may be revealed in open court before a judge or jury and the possible reactions and outcomes such evidence may produce. Also, a clear view of the scope and complexity of the dispute may gauge the public reaction and avoid damage to external relations by finding a mutually satisfying resolution that does not involve a lawsuit.

In the event early resolution of the dispute is not feasible, the pleading phase will typically be followed by a *discovery* period. Here, legal counsel defending the college or university will be tasked with marshaling documents and other tangible materials that may be relevant to the plaintiff's claims and defenses asserted by the institution. The discovery phase involves important proceedings such as deposition, where parties to a lawsuit may be required to appear and respond to questions raised by attorneys representing the defendant or plaintiff. Depositions provide a setting for a person central to a dispute to offer testimony regarding a series of questions under oath. Collectively, the pleadings, deposition transcripts, documents produced during discovery, and related materials constitute the "record" that will be critical to resolution of the lawsuit. The fruits of an effective internal investigation should indeed provide substantial guidance for the discovery phase, especially with respect to identifying witnesses and providing testimony, statements, and reliable evidence that may be dispositive regarding the merits of the lawsuit.

Although television dramas may have many believe that the litigation of the civil lawsuit boils down to dramatic testimony by witnesses in front of a jury, the reality is that most lawyers defending the action of colleges and their administrative team are focused on developing legal arguments that dispose of lawsuits through pretrial motions. The *motion to dismiss* and the *motion for summary judgment* are among the most commonly used pretrial motions used to dismiss lawsuits. A motion to dismiss often is sought during the early stages of the litigation and can also be raised prior to, or in lieu of, the answer. The court may grant a motion to dismiss where the complaint is found legally insufficient, which courts have found to mean that the plaintiff's claims are not plausible. By comparison, the motion for summary judgment is routinely submitted to the court at the close of the discovery period. When granted, summary judgment indicates that the court may dismiss the entire complaint, or certain claims in the complaint, as a matter of law because there is no genuine issue of material fact about which reasonable jurors would disagree.

The internal investigation provides campus decision-makers and legal representatives with valuable information regarding the likely strengths or weaknesses that might accompany a lawsuit brought against a college or university and may be useful in preparing either type of motion. Simply put, the relationship between a pending lawsuit and a campus-driven internal investigation can have significant meaning for the institution's legal defense and assessment of resolution opportunities.

The Risks and Rewards of the Internal Investigation

While the internal investigation provides data, information, and witness statements that may clarify the circumstances regarding student misconduct incidents, the investigation will also scrutinize a college's operations, practices, and the actions of key personnel. Campus administrators and those persons authorizing an internal investigation should understand that in addition to providing advance notice and insights, the investigation may also uncover evidence that the institution or units within the institution have failed to comply with campus policies or their legal obligations. Such troubling findings of fact require immediate action but may be difficult to keep from public disclosure, especially when an investigation reveals that students have been put at risk due to program or administrative failures or unjustified decisions regarding student discipline. In the event such action becomes the subject of a lawsuit, any documents, reports, or materials related to internal investigations may become the focus of discovery requests. Because an internal investigation is likely to come under careful review, it is wise to do it well. Done poorly, it can send a damaging message about the university and its academic programs.

On balance, however, the benefits of the internal investigation outweigh any potential risks for various reasons set out above, such as improving the institution's ability to respond to student misconduct, taking remedial action, and preventing the recurrence of adverse action that may threaten students—the population that essentially drives the higher education process. Their well-being ought never to be taken for granted. Whether students are parties to misconduct allegations, somehow victimized, or just bystanders, their awareness of some wrongdoing—an academic violation or behavioral misconduct—cannot be ignored and must be addressed. The *prompt, internal investigation* signals to students a reason for confidence that the institution's policies and procedures are not empty rhetoric but standards and principles that will be enforced for the good of the campus community and the institution's mission. This book is dedicated to promoting that effort.

Part I

Student Misconduct and the Law

Chapter 1

Constitutional Considerations and Student Rights

Alt-Reich Now* is an activist group that promotes white nationalism and neo-Nazi ideological thinking. In recent months, Alt-Reich Now members have appeared near the Tattnall University campus passing out fliers and inviting white students to attend Alt-Reich Now meetings and events. Student interest in Alt-Reich Now has been minimal, but a small group of students (all white) have embraced the group's message. One student who joined Alt-Reich Now is Nate Bedford. Bedford strongly believes that the organization has a legitimate purpose and has submitted an application to establish a recognized Alt-Reich Now student group dedicated to helping white students avoid incidents of reverse discrimination.

On Saturday, September 12, 2015, Tattnall University hosted a home football game. As students and fans entered the campus to make their way to the stadium, Bedford and about ten other Alt-Reich Now student supporters distributed fliers promoting the

---

*Case studies are fictitious but reports of similar real events are cited in the notes.

organization. Bedford and the other students had not sought permission to distribute their fliers nor did they inform anyone of their intentions to do so. As the Alt-Reich Now supporters passed out fliers they approached several students tailgating, including Steven Carmichael, a leader of the Student Nonviolent Campus Crusade (SNCC), a recognized student organization. SNCC is an anti-racist group dedicated to promoting political activism and social justice to advance equality and non-discrimination. As the two groups converged, Bedford and Carmichael squared off in a heated verbal exchange that turned violent.

According to witnesses at the scene, a fight broke out between the Alt-Reich Now supporters and SNCC students. Reports indicated that during the ruckus Bedford brandished a knife, but no weapon was recovered at the scene. Carmichael suffered no serious injuries but claims that he was attacked by Alt-Reich Now members. The incident was being investigated as a possible hate crime. Tattnall University subsequently commenced a student misconduct investigation regarding the on-campus brawl, the campus climate, the prevalence of racist propaganda, and the on-campus recruitment efforts by white supremacists.[1]

- - - - - - - - - -

Colleges and universities are dynamic institutions. They reflect the composition of the student body, the number and quality of faculty, and the staff employed at a particular campus. These institutions maintain many academic and support programs that function collectively to service a diverse community of students and educators. This complex effort is driven by the mission of the institutions, which can be practically measured by student achievement.

For courts that are compelled to critique the activities of colleges or universities that are involved in litigation as a party or otherwise, it has been acknowledged that "[i]t is the business of a university to provide an atmosphere which is most conducive to speculation, experiment and creation."[2] Moreover, for decades, US courts have described the important contribution educational institutions make to the nation's welfare, characterizing colleges and universities as platforms for faculty and students to engage in rigorous intellectual debate legitimately protected by the federal constitution. In 1960, Supreme Court Justice Potter Stewart stated that "the vigilant protection of constitutional freedoms is nowhere more vital than in the community of American schools."[3] In 1967, Supreme Court Justice William J. Brennan, Jr., wrote: "The classroom is peculiarly the 'marketplace of ideas.' The Nation's future depends upon leaders trained through wide exposure to that robust exchange of ideas which discovers truth 'out of a multitude of tongues, [rather] than through any kind of authoritative selection.'"[4]

Undoubtedly, colleges and universities are tremendous settings for developing the next generation of citizens that will sustain our democratic society and continue the pursuit of a "more perfect Union." In spite of the best efforts of the institutions, however, colleges and universities can also be places where students fall in with the "wrong crowd" or make poor decisions that impact their academic performance. The Alt-Reich Now situation set out above is complicated by issues regarding the racial/ethnic divide, personal prejudice, and a host of legal concerns that implicate free speech, academic freedom, and campus safety. This chapter introduces important constitutional law protections that impact the institution's ability to conduct responsible student misconduct investigations while limiting its exposure to legal liability.

Constitutional Student Protections

A college education has long been valued as the gateway to upward mobility and economic success in the American free market system. The opportunity and access offered to students is put at risk when they get caught up in allegations of behavioral or academic misconduct. Investigations of misconduct can result in sanctions including suspension, expulsion, dismissal, or other penalties that can derail a student's future. Consequently, it is imperative that disciplinary action taken that interferes with any student's pursuit of a degree at the postsecondary level be fundamentally fair and just. This process must begin with an investigatory effort designed to identify the important issues and facts that will allow campus administrators and student affairs personnel to reach justifiable decisions, including sanctions when deemed appropriate.

Weighing the impact disciplinary action can have on students is an important consideration. Therefore the investigation process provides a critical opportunity for the institution to "press pause" and examine the facts and allegations at issue before determining whether disciplinary action is warranted. The need for rules and penalties where violations occur is straightforward and does not require debate. But the more sensitive issue is how college and university administrators resolve conflict and care for students, especially when students have made poor decisions or participated in activities that have put them at risk. Human beings are "imperfect," even on our best days, and generally, college students are still developing (maybe we all are). Young people experience an array of forces that impact their sense of autonomy, maturity, and personal identity. Students often come to college weighed down by the expectations of family and friends. Sometimes they impose benchmark objectives on themselves and struggle to achieve goals on a predetermined schedule.

Students come from every corner of America and various international communities across the globe. Faculty, student affairs personnel, and others across our campuses have struggled to find ways to define or group students in order to serve and educate them. Classifications abound: freshman, sophomore, junior, upperclassman, incoming student, transfer student, night student, student-athlete, graduate student, traditional student, nontraditional student, and on and on. Regardless of their classification, label, or "station in life" (e.g., single, married, parent, military veteran), students can stray from the narrow "degree program" path, lose their way, or simply make mistakes that can jeopardize their education. When student behavior, conduct, or decision-making enters an egregious or counterproductive period, we must ask what is owed to that student. From the perspective of the mission-driven college or university, should the hope that brought the person through the admission process and into the ranks of the student population give way to the uncertain judicial framework, where the classification of "student" is replaced with another label? And if so, are all our students simply one step away from discipline, punitive action, and banishment from the pursuit of a postsecondary education and the higher education experience entirely? In some situations, the answer is yes. Had Gang Lu not committed suicide after shooting several faculty and administrators at the University of Iowa in 1991, his terrible conduct would have deserved the attention of the criminal justice system.[5] But should the same lens be used for the dozens of veterinary students implicated in an online cheating scandal at Ohio State University?[6] In either of these scenarios and in other matters regarding student misconduct, college and university decision-makers are better prepared to act when the prompt, impartial investigation is available as a first option.

The right to pursue an education or earn a degree has been characterized as a property right or a liberty interest. In the frequently cited case of *Dixon v. Alabama State Board of Education*, 294 F.2d 150 (5th Cir. 1961), students expelled for participating in public lunch counter sit-ins and other off-campus demonstrations during a heated period of the civil rights movement filed an action in federal court seeking to have their expulsions overturned. The decision marked an important establishment of students' right to due process where constitutionally protected interests were at stake. Addressing the important private interests that college students have in pursuing higher education at a public university, a federal appeals court noted that "[i]t requires no argument to demonstrate that education is vital and, indeed, basic to civilized society. Without sufficient education the plaintiffs would not be able to earn an adequate livelihood, to enjoy life to the fullest, or to fulfill as completely as possible the duties and responsibilities of good citizens."[7]

Another noteworthy US Supreme Court decision, *Bd. of Curators of the University of Missouri v. Horowitz*, 435 U.S. 78 (1978), considered a medical student's claim that her liberty interest was substantially impaired by an academic dismissal decision based on unsatisfactory clinical performance. The facts presented in the case demonstrated that the faculty at the University of Missouri–Kansas City Medical School fully informed the student that her academic performance was unsatisfactory. Also, observing that her dismissal was based upon academic deficiencies rather than disciplinary misconduct, the Court found that Horowitz's due process rights under the Fourteenth Amendment were not violated even though she was not afforded a formal disciplinary hearing.

The outcomes in *Dixon* and *Horowitz* are almost exclusively influenced by the initial actions taken by administrative decision-makers. *Horowitz* offers important lessons regarding how institutions should respond to students, especially when student disciplinary decisions carry substantial implications. The student in *Horowitz* was nearing completion of her medical degree at the time her academic difficulties surfaced. She had been placed on academic probation and, although some faculty had concerns about her capacity to perform at a satisfactory level, she continued to put forth a reasonable effort. There was even a review of her clinical performance and an oral examination evaluated by several practicing physicians that resulted in divergent conclusions. Two of the doctors involved recommended that the student be allowed to graduate but others disagreed. The decision to dismiss the student was imposed after a careful deliberate review of her academic performance. Despite the student's arguments to the contrary, the Court found that the university administrators and decision-makers did not violate or neglect any constitutional requirements in dismissing her. Furthermore, while the Court acknowledged that even in the cases of minimal disciplinary action students should be given oral or written notice of the charges, an explanation of the evidence that campus authorities have compiled, and an opportunity to present his or her version of the incident, they noted that less stringent procedural requirements apply in academic dismissal cases.[8]

In contrast to the outreach made to the student in *Horowitz*, the students in *Dixon* received little consideration. In *Dixon*, the students were engaged in a noble act of civil disobedience, placing themselves in grave danger as they protested racial segregation by participating in an organized, planned sit-in at a locally owned restaurant in Montgomery, Alabama, that refused to serve black students at the lunch counter. Their action sparked mass demonstrations and resulted in the subsequent expulsion of the students from Alabama State College. While this incident is clouded by the significant social upheaval and political unrest that accompanied the civil rights movement, the concern for the students involved in the alleged misconduct should not be overlooked. The students' dismissal was upheld by the district court but later reversed by the Fifth Circuit for the US Court of Appeals, wherein the court referred to a description of the events related to the student protest including comments offered by the state's governor to the Alabama State College president. "John Patterson, as Governor of the State of Alabama and chairman of the State Board of Education, conferred with Dr. Trenholm, a Negro educator and president of the Alabama State College, concerning this activity on the part of some of the students. *Dr. Trenholm was advised by the Governor that the incident should be investigated, and that if he were in the president's position he would consider expulsion and/or other appropriate disciplinary action.*"[9] The governor's advice to the president is troubling at best. Conducting an investigation of alleged student misconduct has value as an important first step, and the investigative function should not be used as a pretext or a smoke-screen, or merely a prelude to punishment for students who deserved better.

By comparison, the academic administrators in *Horowitz* went beyond their constitutional obligations to demonstrate that the dismissal decision was not arbitrary or capricious. The student was informed of her academic standing and was told that academic dismissal could result if she did not improve her performance. The lesson for those conducting investigations of student misconduct does not simply rest with respect for constitutional standards such as due process but serves as a reminder that an investigation must be a genuine inquiry reaching out to students in difficult times, not a subterfuge for predetermined disciplinary decisions. This does not mean that disciplinary action should not be vigorously imposed. In fact, it is the correct option when it is necessary to protect students from harming others or destabilizing the academic environment. But student misconduct investigations should not be used to camouflage decisions that have already been reached when there is no intention to consider facts, evidence, and information that may be uncovered by an investigation.

The student population, while possessing rights and protections, may become involved in an array of incidents during the course of their educational experience that can lead to disciplinary action. The important task for student affairs and university administrators is the separation of innocent student conduct from conduct or behavior that creates mayhem or represents a danger to others or even to the student herself. Consequently, internal investigation may then be justified for various reasons in some, if not all, situations.[10]

Justifications for Internal Investigations

Reports from Whistleblowers

Just as in the labor and employment context, an individual in an academic setting—including a student witness—who exposes or reports acts of wrongdoing and corruption that represent violations of law, campus regulations, or policy to responsible personnel may be considered a whistleblower.[11] A whistleblower can substantiate a civil claim for retaliation where his or her action represents protected activity for which the whistleblower suffers adverse action and can demonstrate that a causal connection exists between the protected activity and the adverse action.[12] In the college and university context, students can emerge as whistleblowers by virtue of misconduct they witness in academic programs, externship placements, or extracurricular programs. In 2012, students enrolled in a nursing program at London South Bank University were praised by a judge for coming forward to expose patient mistreatment at a hospital.[13] Students coming forward and reporting incidents of wrongdoing should be encouraged because it provides a chance for early intervention and problem-solving, which is in the campus community's best interest (see figure 2).

Criminal and Quasi-Criminal Activity

Internal investigations may also be triggered by allegations that students have engaged in criminal activity.[14] Accusations may come from a variety of on-campus or off-campus sources, and the nature of the alleged student misconduct can involve acts of simple threat or escalate to violence that results in mass shootings. While state and local law enforcement agencies have authority to respond to criminal activity, such egregious conduct usually requires university officials to conduct an investigation to determine potential wrongdoing and how to prevent similar acts of misconduct in the future.[15] Colleges and universities may also elect, based upon the nature and scope of the alleged student misconduct, to partner with outside professionals with the subject matter expertise to investigate and resolve a student misconduct incident.[16]

Preventive Law

While college and university administrators are often confronted with student matters that require prompt attention, preventive law seeks to move beyond a reactionary approach by forming alliances between campus legal counsel, compliance personnel, and other higher education administrators. Academic department chairs and other non-academic managers like student activities directors or residential life personnel and many others should be engaged in the preventive law efforts well before a crisis emerges.[17] Working together, lawyers and campus middle managers should develop goals and strategies that proactively identify legal risk-management approaches that prevent loss or liability to the institution.[18]

Academic Misconduct

Student academic misconduct can emerge from an allegation of plagiarism, which is generally characterized as utilizing the work of another without attribution, or other forms of cheating. At issue in the case of academic misconduct is the integrity of the college or university, its academic programs, and the legitimacy of a student's academic performance. Also, when a student is found to have engaged in academic dishonesty or fraudulent academic practices, an institution may have the authority to revoke academic degrees.[19] Faculty or support personnel such as testing proctors often discover or witness acts of academic misconduct and, therefore, are a valuable source of information for any investigation. Because academic misconduct can result in substantial penalties, a thorough investigation is important to ensure accurate findings regarding alleged misconduct, when misconduct is confirmed, and the imposition of fair penalties.

Regulatory and Compliance Obligations

Compliance programs at colleges and universities are designed to assist the institution by directing employees and staff to conduct their activities in an ethical manner and in compliance with legal and regulatory requirements. Specific areas of legal and regulatory compliance for postsecondary institutions include a complex array of federal and state laws, statutes, rules, and regulations that impact academic programs, governance, business operations, student affairs services, human resources, and numerous other units within the institution. Monitoring the compliance function can often fall to legal counsel, risk managers, compliance officers, internal auditors, or outside consultants who may be called upon to conduct internal investigations to ensure that the institution is taking appropriate administrative action to remain in compliance with these various obligations. Chapter 2 examines in depth the importance of compliance obligations that flow from statutory law and related regulations.

Fiduciary Duty

Somewhat related to regulatory compliance concerns, issues of fiduciary duty should also be considered as a justification for investigatory proceedings. For administrators in higher education, the fiduciary duty concept is understood as embracing a commitment to refrain from fraudulent behavior or self-dealing and instead to act in a diligent, obedient manner, exercising good faith, reasonable care, and prudence with respect to activities on behalf of the institution. Furthermore, executive officers, governance board members, and trustees typically maintain fiduciary duties to exercise care, loyalty, and obedience in the performance of their responsibilities. Conversely, some courts have held that the relationship between an institution and its students is contractual and not fiduciary, while others have recognized the unique dependence students have on a college or university to provide the academic program in good faith and in an accommodating educational environment.[20]

The above-mentioned justifications for internal investigations (see figure 2) do not provide an exhaustive list of reasons that

Figure 2. Justification for the Internal Investigation

may prompt the need for an early inquiry regarding student misconduct. Such a list is probably impossible to develop. The circumstances or activities that have the potential to disrupt or interfere with a student's journey toward graduation are vast and growing. Considering the almost unlimited access students have to computing technology, social media, and other forms of electronic interactions that open the door to unwelcome communication and intrusive behavior, students routinely stand near the gateway to controversy. And, if a student crosses that threshold, colleges and universities must have legitimate internal investigation processes to separate fact and truth from fiction and falsehoods.

Constitutional Protections and the State Action Doctrine

Administrators charged with conducting an investigation of student misconduct must execute the investigation in a manner that does not disregard a student's constitutional rights. The constitutional rights and privileges citizens enjoy are extended to the lives of students matriculating through our nation's institutions of postsecondary education. Whether a student raises a free speech claim protected by the First Amendment, a due process complaint pursuant to the Fourteenth Amendment, or some other allegations safeguarded by a provision of the United States Constitution, it is well-settled that *state action* is a necessary element for any such cause of action to proceed at a public college or university.[21]

The Constitution is highly regarded as a defining document that captures the framework outlining the rights, liberties, and protections that form our democracy. The vast majority of the rights set out in the Constitution are designed as protections against deprivations that may flow from conduct by a state actor. The Constitution functions as a restraint on governmental action or, put another way, action by a state entity where an individual alleges that he or she has been deprived of rights guaranteed by the Constitution. Thus, in order to show a constitutional violation a claimant must be able to demonstrate "state action." The state action doctrine can be triggered by the conduct of governmental officials or private persons acting in concert or at the direction of governmental authority. For instance, some activities are exclusively within the ambit of the state—examples include operating a township or municipality or conducting an election. These activities are public functions and constitute state action. Even private individuals who perform public functions or act in a manner that is considered "entangled" with government regulation may be construed as state actors.

One way to avoid constitutional scrutiny is to select an independent investigator, since his or her work would not be considered state action. Institutions may decide to select an outside entity (law firms, consultants, or investigators) for numerous reasons. The college may determine that certain expertise is needed to analyze the alleged student misconduct, the university may not have the personnel available to conduct the investigation in a timely manner, or the institution may hire an outside firm to conduct the investigation to demonstrate that the process was indeed impartial and objective. Whatever the reason for selecting a private entity to conduct the investigation, it is highly plausible that the work of an independent investigator may avoid constitutional scrutiny because the internal investigation would not constitute state action.

In *Caleb v. Grier*, 598 Fed. Appx. 227 (5th 2015), school officials in Houston, Texas, hired lawyers and private investigators to conduct an internal investigation related to allegations that a former principal and other school employees illegally removed school equipment, misappropriated school property, and participated in a cheating scandal. The plaintiffs—the principal and other school employees—sued, alleging violations of their constitutional rights under the First Amendment as well as claims of freedom of association, retaliation, and due process. The plaintiffs' lawsuit was brought against the school superintendent, the school district, and those hired by the school district—the lawyers and private investigators—to conduct the investigation. The claims against the investigators were dismissed because they were not state actors.

The retention of an outside firm to conduct a student misconduct investigation does not suggest that outside investigators will or should run roughshod over a student's constitutional rights because the investigator may not be held to be a state actor. But understanding the institution's likely exposure as a result of conducting an investigation and the consequences of selecting certain personnel to participate in the investigation places the institution is a stronger position to respond to opposition that may result in reaction to the outcome of an investigation. Furthermore, it is worth noting that for colleges on tight budgets without the resources, or the will, to hire outside professionals to conduct investigations, campus personnel can still be effective but should be prepared to observe and not disregard a student's constitutional rights. For this reason, campus officials charged with internal investigation should receive training and the support necessary to perform the investigation function as well as steer the institution clear of potential legal predicaments.

The US Supreme Court has various tests to determine what conduct is state action. The main question focuses on whether the deprivation of a federal right is caused by the state. More specifically, when a private entity (an external investigator) is involved, did it take decisive steps to cause the plaintiffs' harm or deprivation? In *Caleb*, the court determined that the investigators hired by the public school district did not have the power to discipline and impose adverse employment action on plaintiffs relative to their employment. The investigators did make recommendations on particular issues that the school district was free to consider, act upon, ignore, or reject. Public educational institutions may use their governmental power to commission or facilitate an internal investigation, but where private investigators have no authority over students or ability to impose disciplinary sanctions, private parties cannot take the decisive steps necessary to cause harm and are not state actors.[22] However, a private party can be held liable as a state actor wherein joint action is shown by virtue of an intentional action between the private party and state official.

As for the task of conducting an internal investigation, while institutions may have a practice of investigating matters without the assistance of outside counsel or private investigators, state action will not be found simply because a private entity performs an investigation for a public institution. State entities may elect to have internal investigations performed by private lawyers and others because these are not functions traditionally exclusively reserved to the state. As a practical policy note, campus regulations may or may not explicitly declare what flexibility an institution has to hire a consultant or other professionals to conduct an investigation and the expectations that accompany the retention of such professionals. This is an important consideration for legal counsel and campus administrators to resolve before the need arises to hire an outside investigator. And for questions regarding state action, it is wise for institutions to make clear that decision-making authority to discipline students remains with the college or university at all times and does not transfer to the investigator. Moreover, in the absence of specific policies, campus decision-makers and administrators should be able to articulate the university's general practice regarding various aspects of the internal investigation process, including precautions used to safeguard student rights and constitutional protections.

The First Amendment

The First Amendment to the US Constitution provides that "Congress shall make no law . . . abridging the freedom of speech" and is applicable to the states through the Fourteenth Amendment. As part of the Bill of Rights, which includes the first ten amendments to the federal Constitution, the First Amendment protects and preserves a critical feature of our democracy that extends to students as they pass through our educational institutions. The right to free expression enjoyed by students works in concert with core educational ideals and functions such as learning, teaching, and open dialogue inside the classroom and other forums that are essential to the higher education setting.

But student speech can hardly be confined to predictable forms of expression. In light of the breadth of the First Amendment's free speech clause, restrictions that are content-based and content-neutral (imposed based on the time, place, and manner of speech) give colleges and universities lawful authority to regulate free speech on campus. For student affairs and academic administrators, free speech concerns can stem from campus demonstrations, electronic communication or cyberbullying, controversial speakers visiting the campus, video-surveillance, and even the need to protect speakers and students from each other. Although some expressions are deemed innocuous by-products of college life (for example, students donning humorous symbols and statements on their graduation caps or flashing posters at campus events asking parents to "send money"), other expressions can be viewed as offensive speech.[23]

Of course, the challenge becomes reconciling the important right to "free speech" with the power college officials may have to restrict certain speech on campus. How can administrators know where to draw the line, especially in the area of content-based regulation? It should be noted that the Supreme Court has observed that the First Amendment does not protect categories of speech that incite imminent lawless action, trigger violence, or fall into the categories of defamation, obscenity, or true threats.[24] In the case of true threats, the US Supreme Court has defined speech that is outside the scope of protection under the First Amendment of the Constitution.

"True threats" encompass those statements where the speaker means to communicate a serious expression of an intent to commit an act of unlawful violence to a particular individual or group of individuals. See *Watts v. United States, supra,* at 708, 89 S. Ct. 1399 ("political hyberbole" is not a true threat); *R.A.V. v. City of St. Paul,* 505 U.S., at 388, 112 S.Ct. 2538. The speaker need not actually intend to carry out the threat. Rather, a prohibition on true threats "protect[s] individuals from the fear of violence" and "from the disruption that fear engenders," in addition to protecting people "from the possibility that the threatened violence will occur." *Ibid.* Intimidation in the constitutionally proscribable sense of the word is a type of true threat, where a speaker directs a threat to a person or group of persons with the intent of placing the victim in fear of bodily harm or death.[25]

Certainly, colleges and universities must remain robust testing grounds to examine innovative ideas and competing schools of thought on various topics. But college campuses cannot become fields of nightmares and intimidation. Not the classroom, student union, residence halls, library, or any other campus spaces can be allowed to serve as platforms for student misconduct. But protecting the campus environment from mayhem does not mean that conditions for intellectual dialogue should be sacrificed or thought-provoking discourse discouraged. The evolving call for "safe spaces" on campuses across the country raises challenging issues for student misconduct investigations confronted with allegations that stem from hostile or unwelcome speech.[26] As faculty, students, and administrators endeavor to find the vocabulary to probe the difficult social, political, legal, scientific, and ethical topics of our time, colleges and universities need not feel that their institutions are at the center of a whirlwind with no rudder to guide them. While student protests can turn violent, such protests also can be peaceful and a legitimate exercise of free speech. And although controversial speakers can be disruptive, such speakers also can facilitate spirited debate that is wholly consistent with notions of academic freedom. The challenge is distinguishing legitimate free speech that should be protected and unregulated from speech that embodies a genuine threat. The rise of threat assessment teams can help in this regard.

Threat assessment teams offer a systematic, organized approach to detecting and managing threatening behavior that may breach campus safety.[27] Such teams are often interdisciplinary, comprised of student affairs personnel, campus safety officers, mental health professionals, legal counsel, and others. Among the goals for a threat assessment team are monitoring trends and student concerns on campus, developing and practicing intervention strategies to respond to campus incidents, and educating the campus community about the warning signs that may indicate a threat to the campus community. The assessment function concentrates on distinguishing imminent danger from those incidents that are offensive but fall short of creating a substantial threat to the students, faculty, or staff at the institution. In the case of student unrest, public demonstrations, or events where controversial speech may surface, the threat assessment team provides the college or university with a mechanism to (a) marshal the institution's resources and first responders, (b) assess the threat, if any, posed to the campus community, (c) implement measured or proportional responses designed to neutralize any threat to the institution, and (d) monitor and collect feedback regarding potential or realized threats and evaluate the threat assessment team's performance.

But there remain difficult questions for student misconduct investigators that weigh the importance of student speech against the interests and policies advanced by an institution of higher education. Student misconduct investigations that are triggered by speech or symbolic forms of expression also should spark some consideration for certain guiding legal principles that apply to public colleges and universities that seek to regulate speech. When students exercise their freedom of expression within the campus community, the public forum doctrine has been relied upon to ascertain whether student speech is protected by the First Amendment. "The public forum doctrine arose out of the Court's efforts to address the recurring and troublesome issue of when the First Amendment gives an individual or group the right to engage in expressive activity on government property."[28] Public forum analysis has played an important role in resolving student free expression matters because public colleges and universities are established on government property. However, a leading issue seeks to balance the student free speech interest against the institution's interest in maintaining an academic environment free of material disruptions or substantial disorder.

When investigating student misconduct that may implicate a student's free speech interests, institutions will typically focus on the *content* of the speech or the *conduct* associated with the speech. Content-based restrictions impose limitations on speech based on the subject matter of the speech. However, content-based restrictions are strongly scrutinized by the courts for concerns that governmental officials may engage in censorship or prohibit speech of groups that are unpopular. Conduct related to speech can be regulated by content-neutral restrictions. Content-neutral speech restrictions ignore the subject matter of the speech in question but place limitations on the speech based on the time, place, and manner regulations.

Understanding that a student's speech may be regulated based on the forum within which the speech occurs, the Supreme Court has identified three types of fora: the traditional public forum, the designated public forum, and the nonpublic forum.[29] An institution performing its duties as a state actor has the power to place limitations on free speech depending on the forum from which the speech flows. For instance, streets, sidewalks, and parks represent a "traditional public forum" and state action by a public university to regulate or limit speech in this public forum will receive the highest level of scrutiny. A public college's policies or regulations to limit speech in a traditional public forum must be content-neutral and narrowly tailored to achieve a compelling state interest.

Colleges and universities also may recognize a designated public forum and a limited public forum, which are spaces that have been made available for limited public expression regarding certain subjects. In the designated public forum, the institution may determine the class of speakers allowed in the forum and impose content-neutral time, place, and manner restrictions. For instance, recognized student organizations usually have access to designated public forums, thus providing the opportunity for rigorous open communication on a range of topics. As for the regulation of speech in nonpublic forums, these spaces at universities and colleges are generally not open to public expression and can include administrative offices and facilities where restrictions on speech are considered reasonable and access is granted only to a selected class of speakers.

These methods of regulating speech point toward finding a middle ground between limitless free speech and student expression versus on-campus censorship. Campus internal probes should not neglect student First Amendment rights when investigating students implicated in academic or behavioral misconduct that violates disciplinary policies.

The expanding communication options available to students to exercise their free speech rights raise interesting questions about the right to free expression and what speech is or is not protected by the First Amendment in the college or university environment. To the extent that student affairs administrators acting through their institutions are called upon to investigate student misconduct allegations that implicate free speech rights, an important question will focus on whether the speech is protected by the First Amendment.

Historically, one of the leading US Supreme Court decisions regarding student free speech is *Tinker v. Des Moines Independent Community School District,* 393 U.S. 503, 89 S. Ct. 733, 21 L. Ed. 2d 731 (1969). In *Tinker,* high school students engaged in silent protest by wearing black armbands in opposition to America's military involvement in Vietnam. The students' participation in the antiwar protest came during the turbulence of the 1960s amid the civil rights movement and political unrest. The US Supreme Court's decision in *Tinker* declared that students "do not shed their constitutional rights to freedom of speech or expression at the schoolhouse gate."[30] Also, *Tinker* affirmed the right of students to comment and share their views on controversial issues, if done in a manner that avoids material or substantial interference with the educational environment.

However, where speech does undermine the education mission, the First Amendment right to free speech protection does not grant students an unlimited, absolute protection. Public schools, colleges, and universities are not at the mercy of any and every utterance that a student may express. In *Keefe v. Adams*, 840 F.3d 523, 525 (8th Cir. 2016), a college removed a student from its nursing degree program after receiving complaints about the student's Facebook posts, which demonstrated behavior unbecoming to the profession and transgression of professional boundaries. According to the complaints, the student made statements threatening other students and called a fellow student a stupid b——ch. The accused student countered that his removal from the nursing program violated his First Amendment rights to free speech because the comments were published on the internet outside the classroom and were unrelated to course assignments or requirements.[31] Rejecting the student's First Amendment claim, the court stated that "college administrators and educators in a professional school have discretion to require compliance with recognized standards of the profession, both on and off campus, 'so long as their actions are reasonably related to legitimate pedagogical concerns.'"[32]

The reliance on reasonable compliance standards was also embraced in *Tinker* where the Supreme Court held that school administrators may not randomly silence student speech because students' free speech rights are indeed protected. In another noteworthy case, *Hazelwood Sch. Dist. v. Kuhlmeier*, 484 U.S. 260, 271, 108 S. Ct. 562, 570, 98 L. Ed.2d 592 (1988), the Supreme Court acknowledged that educators maintained authority over school-sponsored publications, theatrical productions, and other expressive activities that students, parents, and members of the public might reasonably perceive as part of the school curriculum, and were not required to support student expression that was inconsistent with the school curricular objectives. The Supreme Court's unwillingness to extend First Amendment protection to speech that materially and substantially interferes with an institution's education operations raises the questions of what speech, symbolic or otherwise, goes too far, especially for cases involving colleges and universities.

College students typically are beyond the age of majority and considered more mature than high school students; thus, speech that substantially interferes with the college environment must reach a higher threshold than what would disrupt the educational goals of a high school. In *Healy v. James*, 408 U.S. 169, 92 S. Ct. 2338, 33 L. Ed. 2d 266 (1972), the Supreme Court disagreed with a decision by a university president to reject a petition by a student organization for official recognition because the administration disagreed with the philosophy of the student group. The Court indicated that the burden of proof to show that the college student organization would substantially interfere with the college environment was on the University, and that refusal to recognize the student group was unconstitutional. As a consequence, a university's content-based restrictions on free speech may indeed be susceptible to First Amendment challenges. For student affairs personnel and college administrators, it is important to have a process to analyze which student speech might garner First Amendment protection and which speech might subject a student to disciplinary action.

When First Amendment free speech issues are raised as part of student misconduct allegations, the internal investigation processes will compel universities and colleges to conduct interviews and gather statements from witnesses with personal knowledge of the events surrounding the alleged incident of student misconduct. Students accused of misconduct may also want to take an active role in preparing their defense or discovering what others may say; however, this is not a free speech concern and the First Amendment does not provide students a right to question or interview others. *Allendale Mut. Ins. Co. v. Bull Data Sys., Inc.*, 32 F.3d 1175, 1177-78 (7th Cir.1994), concludes there is no First Amendment right to "investigate" or to interview witnesses in private. In *Marshall v. Indiana Univ.*, 170 F. Supp.

3d 1201, 1204 (S.D. Ind. 2016), Jeremiah Marshall, a resident assistant and student at Indiana University–Purdue University Indianapolis (IUPUI) was accused of sexually assaulting another student. Marshall was placed on interim suspension and evicted from on-campus housing. Prior to the disciplinary hearing, University officials allowed Marshall to view documents and gave him a witness list but instructed him not to contact persons on the list or other students to testify on his behalf. The hearing panel determined that Marshall was guilty of personal misconduct and he was permanently expelled from the University.

Subsequently, Marshall filed a lawsuit claiming, among other things, that University officials violated his free speech rights because under the federal and Indiana state constitutions he was not allowed to interview students while preparing his defense for the disciplinary hearing. However, the student failed to identify any legal precedent.

> Marshall failed to identify even a single case to demonstrate a recognized free speech right to interview witnesses prior to an educational disciplinary hearing. Instead, he points to cases wherein criminal defendants are afforded the rights to compel and cross-examine witnesses under the Sixth Amendment of the United States Constitution. See, e.g., *Washington v. Texas*, 388 U.S. 14, 18, 87 S. Ct. 1920, 18 L. Ed. 2d 1019 (1967); *Pointer v. Texas*, 380 U.S. 400, 401, 404, 85 S. Ct. 1065, 13 L. Ed. 2d 923 (1965). However, as already discussed, the Seventh Circuit has repeatedly held that a disciplinary hearing in an educational setting is neither a criminal or quasi-criminal hearing. See *Linwood*, 463 F. 2d at 770; *Foo*, 88 F. Supp. 2d at 948-49. As such, the rights afforded to criminal defendants in a criminal trial do not apply. *Id.* Instead, without authority to show that he had a free speech right to interview witnesses on his behalf prior to his disciplinary hearing, Marshall has not pled a viable free speech claim.[33]

Certainly, a college or university may differ as to information and evidence that might be made available to students accused of misconduct. An institution may decide to share information discovered during its internal investigation. However, internal investigations are not criminal or quasi-criminal proceedings, and it is unlikely that a student can justify a First Amendment right to interview fellow students or elicit testimony from others outside an actual disciplinary hearing.

College administrators at practically every type of institution are aware that student speech in the educational environment can or has the potential to become a source of controversy, especially where the speech becomes disruptive, harassing, or promotes counterproductive conduct. And while it is important that the university or college stay true to its mission, these institutions cannot disregard the tightrope that lies between respecting a student's free speech rights and managing varied forms of expression and speech that may emerge from numerous sources.

There can be no source of speech or free expression more challenging than that shared among students through social media. Today's technology has created a platform with practically no parameters or limits on speech. The rise of blogs and online chat rooms along with the capacity to send video and pictures of persons with and sometimes without consent is fraught with opportunities for misconduct and harm to one's personal and professional reputation. This may require some degree of regulation imposed by student affairs administrators.[34] Generally speaking, many of them would probably agree that the technology available to students is far ahead of the administrative techniques and strategies currently developed and available to assess student misconduct that may occur through these new media. While these outlets—Facebook, Twitter, Instagram, and others—have provided a prominent stage for the exchange of ideas, thoughts, or dialogue on any number of intellectual, academic, artistic, or social subjects welcomed in the higher education community, it is naïve and unwarranted to ignore that some expression in the social media space may have negative consequences, including inviting racial bigotry, sexual harassment, or bullying.

Twenty-first century students have made digital communication a part of their identity, and it is not going away. Those charged with investigating student misconduct should be prepared to examine information that may flow exclusively from digital communication sources and/or social media outlets. Institutions differ in their capacity to conduct investigations in this area depending on the availability of computing resources or information technology personnel or overall cost. In some cases, the unwillingness of executive leadership to appreciate the threat posed by social media, electronic communication outlets, or vulnerabilities that the campus computing network may present to the academic environment can undermine the importance of investigating such incidents.[35] Whether the speech emanates from social media platforms or through online messages from student-run social media sites, incidents involving electronic communication represent the new and uncharted frontier for student misconduct investigations.[36]

Appreciation of the potential harm is not enough; the development of practical countermeasures is required. In 2015 the University of Oklahoma found itself in a public firestorm having to respond to a racist chant posted by members of one of the institution's fraternities that went viral over the internet. During the 2016 presidential campaign the networks of the Democratic National Committee (DNC) were hacked resulting in the disclosure of previously thought to be protected emails and voicemail messages, raising troubling questions for the DNC. The lessons from these misadventures are rather clear—try to get in front of the threat.

- Visit or revisit your current policies regarding student free speech and understand what your institution's policies are for expressions that occur via computer usage, social media, and other online platforms and media.

- Determine whether administrators and university counsel have a consistent framework for what constitutes protected speech relative to the fora and university context, whether on or off campus. What is off-campus speech? Does a student using a laptop computer from his apartment ten miles from campus to email X-rated videos related to a sexuality and law class run afoul of policies outlined in the student handbook? Would it make a difference if the student was sending the email message from the university library?
- Have an understanding of why it may be difficult to discipline a student for speech based on content or viewpoint even where the digital or online speech appears controversial or highly offensive. Students will often take to social media to express political opinions and challenge campus officials, and it should be understood that content-based restrictions have frequently received unfavorable review by the courts.
- Create discussion groups and listening sessions that give student affairs personnel an opportunity to discuss social media and student misconduct that materially and substantially interferes with the institution's academic mission and operations. This harkens back to the lesson of *Tinker* respecting the students' free speech rights, without dismissing the notion that speech can go too far. The critical contribution for the internal investigation is finding evidence that shows the requisite on-campus disruption.

The Fourth Amendment

In the course of conducting any internal investigation, the collection of documents, statements from witnesses, and related information are obviously important. For most investigations it will be necessary to interview individuals who have personal information about the events or circumstances that are the subject of the alleged misconduct incident. Also, investigations often call for a search of offices, dormitory rooms, residence halls, student carrels, lockers, and other spaces where students have at the very least a subjective expectation of privacy.

The Fourth Amendment to the US Constitution provides that citizens should be free from illegal searches. More specifically, the Fourth Amendment protects the "right of the people to be secure in their persons, houses, papers, and effects, against unreasonable searches and seizures." Intertwined with the Fourth Amendment protection against an illegal search or seizure is the fundamental right of privacy that citizens maintain as a basic tenet of everyday life. While many—students, parents, and administrators—consider the right to privacy an important value, or even an entitlement, the task of clearly defining the parameters for the right to privacy and the authority for college and university officials to conduct necessary searches can be a challenge.

In addition to searching physical spaces, an investigation may require detaining or searching a student to gather pertinent information or evidence. For instance, in *Reyes v. Central New Mexico Community College,*[37] a student involved in an argument with campus employees that nearly escalated to a physical altercation was subjected to a temporary investigative detention to answer questions about the argument. The student claimed that his Fourth Amendment rights were violated but the court dismissed the claim, finding the investigative detention lasted no longer than reasonably necessary and that the scope did not exceed the underlying purpose of the detention.[38]

The Fourth Amendment applies to action taken by government and is applicable to the states through the due process clause of the Fourteenth Amendment. The prohibition against unreasonable searches and seizures does not as a general matter bar search by government officials but may prompt substantial consequences for illegal searches. Where Fourth Amendment rights are violated an important rule is triggered that can bar lawful consideration of information discovered by what is effectively an illegal search. The "exclusionary rule" prohibits the introduction of evidence obtained unlawfully. Under the exclusionary rule illegally obtained evidence is inadmissible at trial.

This does not suggest that a perfect analogy should be drawn between student discipline and criminal procedure because colleges are not established to enforce criminal law but rather seek to impose standards of conduct consistent with the mission of an educational institution.[39] Nevertheless, student misconduct investigations should acknowledge the Fourth Amendment challenges that may flow from investigative searches. For searches conducted by law enforcement a warrant supported by a probable cause finding is typically necessary, unless the search is permissible within one of the warrantless search exceptions. Courts have widely recognized several exceptions that allow warrantless searches, such as a search incident to a lawful arrest, plain-view searches, and searches where consent is granted to obtain access to premises or information.

An illustration of how an exception to the warrant requirement is applied is found in *Washington v. Chrisman*, 455 U.S. 1, 102 S. Ct. 812, 70 L. Ed. 2d 1087 (1982), wherein a police officer stopped a student carrying a half-gallon of gin and asked the student for identification. The officer accompanied the student to his dormitory room to retrieve his identification. After the student entered the room, the officer observed another student, Chrisman, in possession of marijuana and a pipe on his desk. Chrisman was subsequently charged with possession of marijuana and LSD. The issue before the US Supreme Court was whether the officer violated Chrisman's reasonable expectation of privacy as protected by the Fourth Amendment. Relying on the "plain view" exception to the Fourth Amendment warrant requirement, the Court held that the officer had the right to seize incriminating evidence because he had obtained lawful access to the dormitory room and had a right to remain with the student retrieving his identification.

The Supreme Court has addressed the issue of investigatory searches in the labor and employment context that is instructive for college and university administrators. In *O'Connor v. Ortega*, a hospital employee was placed on administrative leave pending an internal investigation regarding whether the employee engaged in certain workplace misconduct.[40] The investigation involved a thorough search of the employee's office, which he argued violated the Fourth Amendment. The US Supreme Court ruled that public employees have an expectation of privacy in the workplace that may be limited by an employer's practices and procedures.[41] However, employers have an interest that the work of the agency is conducted in a proper and efficient manner, and may conduct work-related misconduct searches that satisfy the standard of reasonableness. Certainly students have some expectation of privacy that must be balanced against the nature and gravity of searches conducted by the institution.

In the context of elementary and secondary schools, the Supreme Court discussed a student search in *New Jersey v. T.L.O.*, 469 U.S. 325, 105 S. Ct. 733, 83 L. Ed. 2d 720 (1985), wherein a female high school student was subject to a search by the assistant vice principal for allegedly violating a school rule. The student's purse was searched, which led to the discovery of marijuana and related items indicating that the student was selling illegal drugs. Finding the search improper, the New Jersey Court excluded the evidence from a juvenile delinquency proceeding on Fourth Amendment grounds. On appeal, the issue before the Court centered on whether the search of the student's purse violated the Fourth Amendment and established the appropriate standard for searches by school officials. The US Supreme Court held that the Fourth Amendment applied to student searches conducted by public school administrators. The legality of such searches depends on reasonableness under the circumstances as determined by a twofold inquiry: first, whether the search was justified at the inception; and second, whether the search was reasonably related in scope to the circumstances that justified the interference in the first place. In this case, school officials searched the student's purse based upon reasonable suspicions that led to the discovery of illegal drug activity.

Thus, the Fourth Amendment provides that where a search or seizure of one's person or dwelling is undertaken in pursuit of a criminal matter our constitutional standard will be controlling. In this criminal scenario, college and university officials are advised to seek a court-granted warrant, which would be issued only upon a showing of probable cause that perhaps a crime has been committed and the student subject to the search is the alleged perpetrator. Where educational administrators implement a search related to internal disciplinary concerns, university officials must remain sensitive to constitutional standards and be clear that their motives to act are consistent with institutional regulations and policies. The best approach may be in the form of full disclosure to students that the institution reserves the right to conduct searches under certain circumstances. Or, perhaps, seeks the consent of students to cooperate with a reasonable search where potential on-campus misconduct is likely. Asking students to acknowledge consent to reasonable searches or including specific language in housing agreements has been viewed as granting university officials permission to conduct searches, especially where health and safety concerns are present.

In *Commonwealth v. Carr*, 458 Mass. 295, 936 N.E. 2d 883 (2010), Boston College police department officers received a report that Daniel Carr and John Sherman might have weapons in their dormitory room and, accompanied by two residence hall directors, they sought to search the students' room. The students were provided a consent-to-search form, which they did not sign, but were advised by the police officer in command at the scene that they wanted to search the room. The search proceeded and the discovery of illegal drugs led to multiple criminal charges against the students. In response, the students filed motions to suppress the evidence, arguing that the search violated the Fourth Amendment because the police did not have a warrant and the students did not consent to the search. The matter eventually reached the Massachusetts Supreme Court, which held that the students did not freely and voluntarily consent to the search and that under the circumstances—confronted by armed police officers and college administrators—an objective person would not have been able to refuse the officers' request to search the room. Hence, the motion to suppress was granted.

However, housing agreements that essentially waive a student's Fourth Amendment right or indicate that a student consents to certain warrantless searches as a precondition to residing on campus should be narrowly drafted and designed to serve institutional purposes. Warrantless campus searches that enforce reasonable health and safety rules will likely not violate the Fourth Amendment, especially when the personnel used to conduct such investigatory searches are not acting on the behalf of or at the direction of law enforcement. For private colleges and universities such Fourth Amendment challenges are doubtful because private institutions of higher education do not engage in state action. But campus police departments at public and private institutions may enter into a memorandum of understanding (MOU) or other agreement with local law enforcement agencies that may bring Fourth Amendment protections into play. In sum, the reach or impact of the Fourth Amendment constitutional provision regarding unlawful searches should not be disregarded by the internal investigation process.

The Fifth Amendment

The Fifth Amendment to the United States Constitution represents a fundamental protection extended to citizens and in pertinent part provides the following: "No person shall be . . . compelled in any criminal case to be a witness against himself, nor be deprived of life, liberty, or property, without due process of law."[42]

The Fifth Amendment grants a citizen the right to refuse to testify or answer questions posed to him or her during a criminal or civil proceeding, formal or informal, where statements made could incriminate an individual in a future proceeding.[43] For investigative proceedings conducted by colleges and universities to determine the veracity and scope of student misconduct incidents, an important question typically centers on whether the Fifth Amendment's privilege against self-incrimination applies to educational institutions. Can students interviewed and/or questioned as part of an institution's internal investigation regarding alleged misconduct refuse to respond by asserting the right to remain silent pursuant to the Fifth Amendment? Courts have offered diverse opinions as to what constitutional protections, if any, extend to college students. The Fifth Amendment makes clear that in a criminal case the accused may refuse to answer questions and that no negative inferences may be drawn from a criminal defendant's silence. However, college students are not criminal defendants and a college or university misconduct investigation falls short of a criminal case.

Nonetheless, student misconduct can result in criminal prosecution and there are legitimate questions that flow from alleged student misconduct that result in disciplinary action by the educational institution as well as criminal charges prosecuted in a court of law that spring from the same circumstances. These situations can indeed grant students protection under the Fifth Amendment privilege against self-incrimination and support the student's right to remain silent.

In *Nzuve v. Castleton State College et al.*, 133 Vt. 225, 231, 335 A.2d 321, 325 (Vt. 1975), a student charged with burglary, attempted rape, and simple assault faced potential expulsion from the College and criminal prosecution in Superior Court. The student responded by seeking to enjoin or delay the College's disciplinary proceeding regarding the expulsion until the disposition of the criminal charges in Superior Court. The student argued that he would be substantially prejudiced in his criminal case if compelled to present his defense and testify in the College's proceedings prior to the criminal court action.

Courts have generally held that colleges and universities need not postpone their disciplinary proceedings until related criminal prosecution has been completed.[44] The law simply does not require that noncriminal proceedings, such as a college or university disciplinary matter, await the resolution of criminal charges.[45] Furthermore, when a student is involved in a college or university disciplinary proceeding and confronted with the decision to testify or provide a statement prior to the resolution of pending criminal charges, the student may choose to remain silent. The Fifth Amendment privilege against self-incrimination prohibits a person from being compelled to be a witness against himself in a criminal case but a campus internal investigation cannot be reasonably construed as a criminal case.

Some courts have chosen not to recognize the right against self-incrimination in student disciplinary matters. In *Goldberg v. Regents of University of California*, several students in good standing at the University of California, Berkeley, became involved in an on-campus protest rally wherein they were arrested and charged with obscenity and violating the peace, which also triggered a university disciplinary proceeding.[46] Student affairs officials notified the students that they would be charged with violating the University's Regulations on Student Conduct and Discipline, and that a special ad-hoc committee would be convened to consider the matter. The committee found that the students' misconduct did constitute a violation of the student conduct regulations and the students charged were suspended or dismissed from the University. The students appealed the disciplinary action but the court held that the University's action was a proper exercise of its inherent general powers to maintain order on campus and to exclude persons detrimental to the University community. Further, the court noted the authority of the University to define the standards and punishments that would prevail in disciplinary proceedings. "[I]n an academic community, greater freedoms and greater restrictions may prevail than in society at large, and the subtle fixing of these limits should, in a large measure, be left to the educational institution itself."[47]

Thus, in the course of pursuing disciplinary action, colleges and universities are not necessarily confined to provide the range of protections available to persons or even students facing criminal prosecution. Educational institutions have a need to execute their own standards to maintain the academic environment. However, colleges and universities are not compelled to escalate their disciplinary processes to anything akin to a criminal prosecution.

But the critical question is whether statements provided in a student misconduct investigation may be used later against the student in criminal prosecution. Courts have held that students may assert the Fifth Amendment privilege against self-incrimination in certain circumstances, relying on the US Supreme Court decision in *Garrity v. New Jersey*, 385 U.S. 493, 87 S. Ct. 616, 17 L. Ed. 2d 562 (1967). In *Garrity*, the Supreme Court established that the government may not use self-incriminating statements that were compelled by the threat of job termination, in this case of police employees. The police officers in the case were interviewed as part of a state investigation into the fixing of traffic tickets; they were told that if they refused to testify they would be removed from office. The testimony given in the internal investigation was later introduced against them in a criminal trial, which resulted in their convictions. The convictions were later reversed by the US Supreme Court because the officers' testimony given during the investigation was *compelled* and held inadmissible in violation of the Fifth Amendment.

Applying this reasoning to a student misconduct investigation, if a student is forced or otherwise compelled to answer incriminating questions during an investigation to avoid disciplinary action, such incriminating statements would be inadmissible in a subsequent criminal proceeding because the student's statement or testimony and fruits of such testimony would be by compulsion.[48] At some institutions, the right to remain silent without the threat of an adverse inference is set out in student handbooks or student policy manuals along with the right to consult counsel, the right to present evidence and witnesses, and the right to appeal any final decision.[49] Where the right to remain silent is well defined in an institution's policies and procedures, it is unlikely that a Fifth Amendment issue will arise. Students who voluntarily elect to answer questions with knowledge of their rights are not compelled and the Fifth Amendment does not apply. However, students who choose to remain silent or refuse to answer questions during a university investigation effectively forfeit the opportunity to control the direction of the investigation, which may have serious consequences as well.[50] For some institutions, this approach may raise a fairness concern that can be resolved by assuring students who choose to remain silent that no adverse inference will be drawn from the decision. The Fifth Amendment does not prohibit or bar student disciplinary investigative proceedings, however, where investigators or university officials compel students to answer questions or give testimony, and if their statements are characterized as involuntary, they will be inadmissible in a future criminal proceeding.

The Fourteenth Amendment

Section one of the Fourteenth Amendment to the Constitution, perhaps the most frequently cited provision of the Constitution relative to higher education, states, in part, that "[n]o State shall . . . deprive any person of life, liberty, or property, without due process of law." Due process is ultimately viewed as a call for fundamental fairness in our democracy and embodies two aspects: substantive due process and procedural due process. *Substantive due process* provides that a student may not be deprived of life, liberty, or property through arbitrary and capricious disciplinary decisions that may interfere with a student's interest in continuing his or her education or pursuing a degree program. *Procedural due process* provides that students are granted the opportunity to defend themselves against any alleged wrongdoing prior to action by student affairs administrators or others to discipline or adversely impact the student's property or liberty interest to higher education.

In *Guse v. University of South Dakota*, 2011 WL 1256727 (D. S.D. 2011), a student dismissed from the University's audiology program claimed that her substantive due process rights were violated because the University's decision to dismiss her was not careful and deliberate. Discussing the requirements for a substantive due process claim, the court noted that a student objecting to disciplinary action must make a two-part showing: "(1) that she had a property or liberty interest; and (2) there was not a rational basis for the adverse decision."[51] In *Guse*, there was agreement that the student had a property or liberty interest in continued enrollment in the audiology degree program. As for part two, the student had to show that the dismissal was arbitrary and capricious. The phrase "arbitrary and capricious" is a familiar term, denoting hasty and perhaps haphazard decision-making; but its meaning does have some precision. Specifically, decisions of this nature have no rational basis and can be motivated by bad faith without regard to a student's academic performance. Further, student disciplinary decisions that are deemed arbitrary and capricious often are found to have been handled differently than other similar student cases and result in decisions that are not based on careful and deliberate action.[52]

Colleges and universities can satisfy the careful and deliberate standard by ensuring that student disciplinary decisions are based on substantial evidence. A record of substantial evidence can be best produced by conducting a thorough, independent investigation that demonstrates (a) whether disciplinary action is necessary and (b) that any discipline imposed conforms to current legal standards and established institutional disciplinary policy and procedures. In *Guse*, the court denied the University's motion for summary judgment because an independent investigation was not conducted determining that the academic dismissal decision was careful and deliberate. Serious concerns were raised regarding whether the University decision was reasonable or that the student's due process rights were granted in full. To avoid such challenges, consider the following suggestions:

Do not make a student misconduct investigation into a "gotcha" exercise. A student misconduct investigation cannot turn into *The Hunt for Red October.*[53] Yes, students are a reflection of society and can operate with ill intent; however, the lens of the college or university decision ought not to be overly clouded by a view of students as potential troublemakers. If that's the situation, then an institution's security mechanisms should be alerted and any threat should be swiftly dealt with. However, student affairs and academic administrators should begin with the premise that every student admitted to the institution should be given a reasonably wide avenue to complete the academic program. And any investigation into student misconduct must be fair, impartial, and focused on corrective actions, not punishment.

Avoid a rush to judgment. Student misconduct incidents often obligate student affairs personnel and other administrators to act quickly, to de-escalate situations that put students at risk, and to provide answers to difficult questions that may impact a student's future or prevent an unfortunate recurrence. While promptly addressing the alleged misconduct is important and avoiding unnecessary delay is vital, an investigation cannot spiral into a hasty exercise that tramples—or is perceived to trample—upon a student's due process rights. The reality is that a student misconduct investigation can be efficient and effective, but it will take some time to perform and is often dictated by the number of persons involved and the overall complexity of the incident. Given these circumstances, college and university decision-makers should remain careful in their fact-gathering and deliberative processes and avoid a rush to deliver findings that are not supported by substantial evidence. As an alternative, reasonable timetables should be developed with frequent updates to inform concerned parties that the matter is receiving prompt attention.

Create an atmosphere that encourages students to come forward. Bad news and rumors can and may travel rapidly among the student body. Electronic communication, social media, and the old-fashioned inability to resist spreading gossip are all likely to provide certain segments of the student population with some information about a student misconduct incident. Of course, not all matters will become public knowledge or a subject on someone's Facebook page: a plagiarism allegation that surfaces at the end of the academic year is likely to get less attention than a brawl among students during a flag football game sponsored by the recreation center.

Regardless of the situation, how the institution manages a student misconduct incident will influence whether students come forward with helpful information or withhold relevant knowledge or evidence. Creating an atmosphere that encourages students to come forward during an internal student misconduct investigation starts long before an incident occurs. A sense of community should be cultivated among students that minimizes concerns that students may suffer retaliation or other negative consequences for coming forward. Also, with the input of legal counsel, consideration should be given to options that allow students to share information anonymously or in private conference settings.[54]

Appreciate the distinction between disciplinary and academic misconduct. No two investigations are the same, and there are subject matter differences between investigations regarding student misconduct. Matters involving academic integrity present challenges that are distinct from matters involving behavioral misconduct. Academic issues may involve testing procedures, the exam administration processes, action taken by proctors, instructor bias, disability accommodations, plagiarism, etc. Behavioral misconduct can involve assault, violence, or even conduct that can threaten public safety. Therefore, colleges and universities are advised to build the capacity to investigate a diverse range of student misconduct matters.

The freedoms and civil liberties that embody America as expressed through the federal Constitution are not diminished but recognized and respected by the collegiate experience. However, the US Supreme Court has indicated in numerous decisions that the constitutional protections available to all citizens, including college students, can coexist with appropriate levels of discretion that colleges and universities require to preserve and promote higher education.

Chapter 2

Statutory Law and Avoiding Investigatory Mishaps

Shannon and David, both students at Buckley University (BU) in Taylor, Georgia, have been dating for over a year. They are in love and hope to spend their lives together as they pursue rewarding careers after graduation. About a month ago, early in the semester on a typical Saturday night, Shannon and David decided to check out the night life in their college town. They spent the evening eating hot wings and drinking beer at a popular sports bar a few blocks from campus. The bar crowd includes lots of students as well as folks from the local community. As the evening progressed, David excused himself to visit the restroom. While he was away, a stranger approached Shannon and offered to buy her a drink. She promptly refused, explaining "I'm with my boyfriend." The stranger replied, "Well, maybe that's your problem, you need a *man*-friend" as he attempted to place his hand on her shoulder. Insulted, Shannon again indicated her lack of interest. The exchange became heated, and when David emerged from the men's room he found the stranger pointing a finger at Shannon and calling her a "stuck-up prima donna."

David immediately got between Shannon and the stranger, and within minutes the two were pushing and shoving. A brawl ensued between the two men that spilled outside the sports bar, where Shannon picked up a bottle and hit the stranger on the head. Shortly thereafter, David and the stranger were pulled apart by others and the fight was broken up.

The following Monday, Shannon returned to classes at BU. At the same time, a local police officer from the Taylor Police Department (TPD) was also on campus. The stranger from the Saturday night brawl had filed a police report claiming that he had an argument with David and Shannon and that Shannon attempted to cause him serious bodily harm by striking him on the head with a blunt object with deadly and/or reckless intent. With a warrant for Shannon's arrest in hand, the police officer requested her class schedule from the BU Registrar's Office. The registrar was reluctant to release any information to the TPD officer for two reasons: (1) she was concerned that FERPA requires her to protect the student's information from disclosure; and (2) she was worried about the lasting harm that might befall Shannon if she were publicly handcuffed and ushered off campus in police custody in front of her classmates and dozens of other students.

Historically the US Congress has taken steps to aid and protect students numerous times. In 1944, Congress passed the Serviceman's Readjustment Act, commonly known as the G.I. Bill. One of its many benefits was a provision to pay tuition and living expenses to students attending college or vocational schools. Congress worked on behalf of students again, in 1958, when it passed the National Defense Education Act. This act, a direct response to the Soviet Union's success with the launch of *Sputnik 1,* was intended to encourage American students to study science and technology by offering low-interest loans to those majoring in math or science.

In the 1970s, Congress again took action to benefit America's students—this time by protecting their privacy and safety and by prohibiting discrimination. Title IX, a federal civil rights law, was passed as part of the Education Amendments of 1972. It is designed to prohibit discrimination based on sex at colleges and universities receiving federal financial assistance. The Family Educational Rights and Privacy Act of 1974 (FERPA) protects a student's educational records from random disclosure. And more recently, the Jeanne Clery Disclosure of Campus Security Policy and Campus Crime Statistics Act (Clery Act), signed in 1990, compels institutions of higher education to collect and report information that impacts student safety. The public policy thread that weaves through each of these statutory provisions has a profound impact on student life, and in many situations, the student misconduct investigation.

FERPA

Student affairs administrators or other designated professionals charged with the investigation of student misconduct matters are routinely confronted with gathering information that verifies or debunks allegations within the scope of the student misconduct investigation. In the search for reliable information that clarifies unanswered questions, it is critical to recognize that students have certain privacy protections that are supported by federal law. Since 1974, the Family Educational Rights and Privacy Act, 20 USC § 1232g (FERPA), has protected the privacy interests of students and their parents by limiting the transferability of students' educational records without their consent. Also known as the Buckley Amendment in reference to its leading sponsor, Senator James Buckley of New York, FERPA has represented a step forward in curtailing the unauthorized disclosure of personal or identifiable student information in educational records in the absence of a student's consent.[1] Enacted pursuant to the spending clause in Art. I, §8 of the US Constitution, FERPA functions as a precondition, whereas Congress provides funds to educational institutions on the condition that such agencies or institutions decline to adopt a policy or practice permitting the release of education records or personally identifiable information of students without the written consent of the students or their parents.[2]

FERPA provides specific rights to an "eligible student," defined as a person 18 years of age or older or who attends a postsecondary institution. The rights afforded college students include the authority to inspect, review, and request amendment of a student's educational record and the right to provide consent prior to the disclosure of personally identifiable information. An education record as defined by FERPA refers to the following:

> [T]hose records, files, documents, and other materials which . . . (i) contain information directly related to a student; and (ii) are maintained by an educational agency or institution or by a person acting for such agency or institution (20 U.S.C. § 1232g(a)(4)(A)).

Education records do not include:

> (i) records of instructional, supervisory, and administrative personnel and educational personnel ancillary thereto which are in the sole possession of the maker thereof and which are not accessible or revealed to any other person except a substitute; (ii) records maintained by a law enforcement unit of the educational agency or institution that were created by that law enforcement unit for the purpose of law enforcement; (iii) in the case of persons who are employed by an educational agency or institution but who are not in attendance at such agency or institution, records made and maintained in the normal course of business which relate exclusively to such person in that person's capacity as an employee and are not available for use for any other purpose (20 U.S.C. § 1232g(a)(4)(B)).

The congressional action that led to the enactment of FERPA points directly to the obligation educational institutions have to respect the privacy of students. In the context of a student misconduct investigation and subsequent litigation that may result from a campus internal investigation it is important to know what FERPA requires regarding access to a student's educational records. The possibility that the interests of a college or university regarding a student misconduct investigation could collide with the FERPA protections afforded to student educational records is indeed real. Hence, although FERPA does not use terms such as "privileged" or "confidential," courts have acknowledged a federal policy prohibiting the release of student educational records absent proper consent.[3] In the event a student is unwilling to consent to the release of his or her education records, FERPA does permit disclosure in certain situations. For instance, an exception to FERPA allows the disclosure of personally identifiable student information where disclosure is authorized by subpoena or a court order.[4] But federal regulations do require that educational institutions make a reasonable effort to notify students or parents prior to the disclosure, thereby providing an opportunity for the student or parent to seek a protective order to quash or modify the subpoena or court order. Further, the release of education records protected by FERPA could be overridden by other legal standards, such as requirements that Title IX supersedes any conflicting FERPA provision.[5] An educational institution also may disclose the final results of a disciplinary proceeding conducted by a postsecondary institution wherein the student is the alleged perpetrator of a crime of violence or non-forcible sex offense.[6]

Let's consider the hypothetical scenario at the beginning of this chapter. FERPA provides that an educational institution may not disclose personally identifiable information from a student's education record unless the information is directory information, the student consents to the disclosure, or the disclosure is permitted under a FERPA exception.[7] Shannon's class schedule may not be academic information such as a written exam or transcript, but nonacademic information such as class schedules, disciplinary records, and financial aid records are also part of a student's education record.[8] Such information would not fall within the definition of directory information and could not be released to the police officer without Shannon's consent. As noted above, there is a FERPA exception that allows disclosure of education records that comply with a judicial order or subpoena. It is unlikely that a warrant for Shannon's arrest could be construed as a judicial order or subpoena. Also, FERPA does have a health and safety exception that would grant the police access to a student's education record. While the bar brawl appears to have been an isolated incident, if Shannon represented a public safety threat the police officer would likely be able to gain access to her education records.[9]

It is important to note that campus officials are not granted automatic access to student educational records. For student misconduct investigations, FERPA does grant access to student educational records, allowing nonconsensual disclosure to a student's educational records where school officials (that can include professors, administrators, and legal counsel) have a legitimate educational interest.[10] While no bright-line rule defines "legitimate educational interests," commentators have discussed the meaning in broad, functional terms. "A 'legitimate educational interest' can be broadly defined to include any circumstance in which the school 'official' needs the information in order to do his or her job on the school's behalf."[11] In *Medley v. Bd. of Educ., Shelby Cty.*, 168 S.W.3d 398, 405 (Ky. Ct. App. 2004), a teacher agreed to have cameras installed in her classroom to videotape her teaching in response to student complaints. Subsequently, the teacher asked to view the videotapes to examine her teaching and classroom management. The school refused to allow the teacher access to the videotapes, claiming that viewing the videotapes was prohibited by FERPA. Reversing a lower court decision, the Kentucky Court of Appeals indicated that the videotapes did constitute educational records but that FERPA expressly permitted viewing education records by a teacher, so long as a legitimate educational interest is established.

Whether FERPA serves as a federal tool, or even a privilege, to prevent disclosure of student records was at issue where an Idaho State University (ISU) graduate student raised a national origin discrimination claim.[12] Jun Yu, a graduate student pursuing a PhD in Clinical Psychology claimed that he was dismissed from the doctoral program in violation of Title VI of the 1964 Civil Rights Act, 42 U.S.C. § 2000d *et seq.* In support of his lawsuit, the plaintiff graduate student sought the student records of all students pursuing the doctoral degree between 2008 and 2015 to prove that as an Asian student he was treated differently than non-minority students, in violation of Title VI standards. Among the defenses asserted by the University, ISU argued that the plaintiff failed to satisfy the significantly higher burden required by FERPA as compared to the relevance standard set out under Rule 26(b)(1), which allows parties to obtain documents under the Federal Rules of Civil Procedure. Specifically, with regard to the graduate student's request for educational records, the federal district court stated the following:

> The Court finds the records requested by Plaintiff are relevant to his claim of discrimination based on national origin and his allegations at this stage in the proceedings are sufficient to warrant production of these materials. Plaintiff's need for these records sufficiently outweighs the students' privacy interest, when such interests are otherwise protected through alternative means. In that regard, the Court sees no reason for the identifying information of the other students be disclosed, other than as to nationality and ethnic origin, if known. The parties are ordered to attempt to reach agreement in good faith upon appropriate redactions to the information contained in such records, the use of the records, and the limited distribution and protection of such materials, along with provisions for their return.[13]

Hence, the lesson for student misconduct investigations is that educational record may not entirely rely on FERPA as a bar to access. School officials with legitimate educational interests or litigants who can show that their need for student documents outweigh another student's privacy interest may indeed be able to overcome FERPA protections. This is especially the case where alternative means exist to limit disclosure of student identifying information by appropriate redactions or other methods. Nevertheless, given the likelihood that legal challenges from an internal investigation will identify or even publicize the names of students who may be implicated in acts or alleged acts of misconduct, college and universities must remain diligent and should make every effort to anticipate potential privacy concerns and the impact of FERPA.

The Clery Act

Few topics in higher education have become more prominent in recent decades than the challenge to improve campus safety at our colleges and universities. The Crime Awareness and Campus Security Act of 1990, also known as the Jeanne Clery Disclosure of Campus Security Policy and Campus Crime Statistics Act (Clery Act), 20 USC § 1092(f), has been a leading legislative enactment designed to advance campus security.[14] This federal statute obligates postsecondary institutions to report crimes that include murder, robbery, aggravated assault, and motor vehicle theft and make statistical information available to the public. Further, in March 2013, the Campus Sexual Violence Elimination Act (Campus SaVE Act) was enacted as part of the Violence Against Women Reauthorization Act of 2013 (VAWA), which amended the Clery Act.[15] The Clery Act and the Campus SaVE Act have sought to increase transparency and advance reporting, responsiveness, and prevention education programs regarding incidents of sexual violence. VAWA, as amended, requires colleges and universities to report crimes of domestic violence, dating violence, stalking, and sexual assault in addition to the crimes already required to be reported under the Clery Act.[16] These laws and accompanying regulations expand the rights granted to victims of sexual violence and represent a national effort to put an end to sexual assault at American colleges and universities.

Title IX

The fight against prejudice and unlawful discrimination in American life significantly predates the passage of Title IX of the Education Amendments of 1972, 20 U.S.C. §1681 *et seq.* (Title IX)[17] or other legislative efforts designed to level the playing field for women, persons of color, or others in our society. Whether one considers the language in the Declaration of Independence crafted by the country's founding fathers that "all men are created equal" or President Lincoln's poignant reminder in his 1863 Gettysburg Address that the nation was "conceived in liberty, and dedicated to the proposition that all men are created equal," the quest for equality has long been a national struggle.[18]

Perhaps no phase of the campaign for fundamental fairness and equality under the law has had a more profound impact on American higher education than the civil rights movement, which challenged racial discrimination on moral and legal grounds. Among the many achievements of the civil rights movement, passage of the Civil Rights Act of 1964 represented an enormous step forward for citizens previously denied basic privileges and rights because of their race, color, national origin, or sex.[19]

As the civil rights movement played out across the country, college and university campuses served as important stages for political and social protest. Topics such as racial discrimination, the Vietnam War, poverty, and gender equality came under tremendous scrutiny, and congressional lawmakers were compelled to act. The passage of Title IX of the Education Amendments in 1972 stands as perhaps the nation's premier legislative achievement in the effort to attain gender equity and eradicate sex discrimination in educational programs. At its core, Title IX provides that no person, on the basis of sex, shall "be excluded from participation in, be denied the benefits of, or be subjected to discrimination under any education program or activity receiving Federal financial assistance" 20 U.S.C. § 1681(a). Notably patterned after the 1964 Civil Rights Act, Title IX has for decades sought to make clear that sex discrimination has no place in American higher education.[20] Whether applied to advance gender equity in intercollegiate athletics or to the effort to stamp out sexual violence on college and university campuses, Title IX strives to eradicate discrimination, harassment, and violence based on sex by specifying that colleges and universities issue policies against sex discrimination and establish procedures for prompt and equitable resolution of sex discrimination complaints.

For public and private institutions of higher education that are the recipients of federal funding, Title IX and the Department of Education's Office for Civil Rights (OCR) seek to prohibit sexual harassment in education programs or activities. As an administrative enforcement agency, the OCR is authorized to take action against recipient institutions that fail to comply with the law. More specifically, OCR is vested with the authority to conduct investigations, perform compliance reviews, and provide technical assistance to prevent discrimination in educational programs receiving financial support from the US Department of Education. Also, OCR seeks to advance compliance with the Title IX prohibitions against sexual harassment, sexual assault, and gender-based discrimination by publishing guidance and related information.[21] Offered as a guidance document or a "Dear Colleague Letter," OCR provides extensive commentary for higher education administrators and legal counsel to consider related to obligations and requirements under Title IX.[22] However, it is important to note that courts have often held that OCR guidance is not binding legal authority and that OCR has on its own authority taken action to withdraw its guidance. On September 22, 2017, the Department of Education unilaterally withdrew the Dear Colleague Letter on Sexual Violence issued by OCR on April 4, 2011, and the Questions and Answers on Title IX and Sexual Violence issued by OCR on April 29, 2014.[23]

OCR has offered numerous practical steps for investigations of alleged Title IX misconduct at institutions of higher education such as the following:[24]

- Colleges and universities must adopt and publish grievance procedures that notify students and employees where to file a Title IX complaint and the steps that will be taken to notify an alleged perpetrator of the factual basis for the alleged charges.
- An investigation of a Title IX complaint must be prompt, impartial, adequate, and reliable, granting parties the opportunity to identify witnesses and other evidence, as well as the chance to examine and respond to evidence supporting a victim's allegations of sexual misconduct. Among these considerations, perhaps the most important to manage involves confirming that the investigator is impartial. While substantial attention is routinely given to reviewing the investigator's professional credentials and reputation, affirmative steps should also be taken to determine that the investigator or the investigation team has no conflicting activities, obligations, or dealings that would undermine the legitimacy of the investigation or its findings. Therefore, a conflicts check should be executed at the outset of an investigation and repeated as needed based on the scope of the investigation.[25]

Congress designed Title IX to prohibit a range of intentional gender-based misconduct by embracing a broad view of what would constitute discriminatory behavior. See *Jackson v. Birmingham Bd. of Educ.*, 544 U.S. 167, 125 S. Ct. 1497, 161 L. Ed.2d 361 (2005); *Bougher v. Univ. of Pgh.*, 713 F.Supp. 139, 143-44 (W.D. Pa.1989) (a Title IX plaintiff must show that he or she was subjected to discrimination in an educational program that receives federal assistance). Further, in two important Supreme Court cases, *Gebser v. Lago Vista Independent School District*, 524 U.S. 274, 277, 118 S. Ct 1989, 1993, 141 L.Ed.2d 277 (1998) (teacher-on-student harassment) and *Davis v. Monroe County Bd of Educ.*, 526 U.S. 629, 650, 119 S. Ct 1661, 143 L.Ed.2d 839 (1999) (student-on-student harassment), the Court announced liability standards for cases where private actions for money damages were sought under Title IX. To assert a private cause of action under Title IX, a plaintiff must show that the recipient educational institution (1) had actual knowledge of the alleged sexual misconduct, (2) was deliberately indifferent to the known sexual misconduct, (3) that the victim-student was subjected to severe, pervasive, and objectively offensive misconduct based on sex, (4) that the student's educational experience was undermined, and (5) that the plaintiff-victim was denied access to educational benefits or opportunities. See *Simpson v. Univ. of Colorado Boulder*, 500 F.3d 1170, 1176 (10th Cir. 2007).

Because colleges and universities have a compelling reason to prevent sex discrimination and comply with Title IX, campus administrators should be familiar with the law's enforcement structure and prohibition regarding discriminatory conduct for all educational programs or activities as set out by the federal regulations. Specific prohibitions expressed in the federal regulations at 34 C.F.R. § 106.31(b)(1)-(7) provide that educational institutions receiving federal financial assistance shall not differentiate, separate, deny, or otherwise limit any aid, benefit, or service to a student on the basis of sex.[26]

Title IX aims to protect institutional employees, staff, and students from various forms of sexual discrimination, including sexual violence and harassment. When an institution knows or reasonably should know of conduct that violates Title IX, the college or university must take immediate and appropriate action to investigate the matter. The law does not impose a one-size-fits-all process for conducting a Title IX investigation. However, in *Doe v. Brown University*, a sexual misconduct case that involved the review of a university's investigative procedure, the court observed the "investigator model" used to investigate Title IX claims:

> Brown [University] also adopted a new Complaint Process Pursuant to the Title IX Policy ("Complaint Process") (Ex. 3), which delineates the procedures for the receipt, investigation, and informal and formal resolution of complaints alleging student sexual misconduct (Trial Tr., vol. II, 4:5-24, ECF No. 52). Unlike the previous model where evidence was presented directly to a hearing panel, the new Complaint Process uses an "investigator model" for handling sexual misconduct cases (Trial Tr., vol. I, 38:1-12, ECF No. 51). Under this model, there is a single investigator, whose role is to gather "information through interviews of the complainant, respondent, and witnesses and synthesize the information in a report" (Complaint Process 3, Ex. 3). "The investigator has the discretion to determine the relevance of any witness or other evidence and may exclude information in preparing the investigation report if the information is irrelevant, immaterial, or more prejudicial than informative" (*Id.*). The Complaint Process dictates that "[t]he investigator's report will include credibility assessments based on their experience with the complainant, respondent, and witnesses, as well as the evidence provided" (*Id.* at 4). However, it also states that "[t]he investigator will not make a finding or recommend a finding of responsibility" (*Id.*). The investigator model has become increasingly popular among colleges and universities, particularly "peer institutions of Brown."[27]

Many investigations can have a similar structure but in practice the investigation process will often vary depending on the nature of the allegation, the student or students involved, the size and administrative structure of the institution, as well as the impact of state or federal law, including what the institution has learned from past experiences. Further, colleges and universities must conduct Title IX investigations in a manner that is consistent with federally guaranteed due process rights.[28] While an institution has flexibility regarding the structure of the investigation, the process should focus on implementing a fair and balanced fact-finding effort granting complainant and the alleged perpetrator the opportunity to share pertinent information without violating either individual's due process rights.

In 2014, a White House task force issued a report identifying what should be done to ensure that victims of sexual violence were supported and that institutions of higher education understood the obligation to take action when these incidents occurred.[29] In April 2015, OCR issued federal guidance for Title IX Coordinators to clarify the role and responsibilities of the position and to expound upon the obligations the Title IX Coordinator has to help the institution comply with the law.[30] In 2017, the Department of Education announced the release of new interim Questions and Answers guidance for colleges and schools on how to conduct investigations of campus sexual misconduct under federal law.[31] Hence, the call to action for colleges and universities to respond to sexual misconduct allegations is difficult to overstate, and Title IX's legal landscape is growing increasingly complex for student affairs personnel, administrators, legal counsel, and professionals charged with investigating sexual assault claims. Therefore, investigators approaching Title IX student misconduct allegations should recognize that these incidents occupy a unique space that requires specialized preparation and considerations.[32]

Other Claims and Mishaps That May Undermine an Investigation

An overriding objective of any internal investigation is to discover, verify, and minimize misconduct that interferes with the student's matriculation through his or her degree program or is contrary to the institution's academic mission. As explained above, observing constitutional and statutory law is a prerequisite for student affairs personnel and administrators at every level within the institution. But the actions taken by persons directly and indirectly involved in the investigation are also critical and, if improper, can derail or undermine the investigation. For administrators and other decision-makers at colleges and universities who may have a role in an internal investigation proceeding, every effort should be made to avoid negligent action and related forms of investigatory misconduct or malfeasance. College and university administrators should embrace a commitment to refrain from fraudulent behavior or self-dealing and to act in a diligent, objective manner, exercising good faith, reasonable care, and prudence with respect to activities undertaken on behalf of the institution.[33] More specifically, student misconduct investigations should adhere to the tenets and considerations that may avert federal or state law challenges regarding the institution's investigative action. Consider the following guidelines:

Incorporate a nondiscriminatory, anti-retaliation commitment into the investigation process. Witnesses, complainants, person's accused of wrongdoing, and others involved in the investigation should be treated in an ethical and professional manner throughout the process. At no point during the investigation should race, sex, religious beliefs, mental or physical disability, or other illegitimate classifications influence the proceedings. Furthermore, parties to the investigation should be notified in clear terms that the institution prohibits retaliatory action and that their involvement will not result in unlawful repercussions.

Delay prematurely establishing a theory of the incident under investigation and discrediting witnesses prior to their interview. While student misconduct matters vary in terms of their scope and gravity, whether the incident involves a matter of plagiarism or gun violence on campus there is likely to be a wide range of information and commentary available surrounding the matter from on-campus and off-campus sources. Evaluate the information or commentary regarding an alleged incident to determine if it constitutes anything more than misinformation from an unreliable source. Given this possibility, it is imperative that the investigation resist any temptation to "rush to judgment" and instead, allow the investigation process to remain a discovery and learning experience. Yes, the investigation should be efficient, well-managed, and goal-driven, but at the same time, it must be thorough and rigorous, eschewing unreliable information.[34]

Avoid surreptitiously recording without consent. There is nothing inherently problematic about using an electronic device to audibly record a statement or testimony offered by a witness. Recording devices are frequently used in federal and state court proceedings, administrative hearings, and at the pretrial stage that may include depositions and witness interviews. However, internal investigations are not formal court proceedings and are often commenced to avoid civil or criminal litigation. Where recording devices are used it is the best practice to have the parties involved voluntarily consent to being recorded. Various states have imposed laws regulating the circumstances under which persons may or may not be recorded without consent.[35] The significance of audio or video recordings may be compelling in student misconduct matters, but improper or illegally recorded and/or obtained statements or images can jeopardize an investigation.[36]

Do not make extensive demands for information if it is not reasonably necessary based on the scope and goals of the investigation. Especially in cases where a student claimant comes forward with allegations that he or she has been victimized or subjected to inappropriate treatment, investigators and student affairs personnel should operate under the presumption that the student is acting in good faith, unless there are overriding reasons to question the veracity of the complaint. Nonetheless, at no point during the investigation should complainants, witnesses, or persons accused be threatened or forced to provide documents, records, information, or items as part of the investigation. Nor should parties to the investigation be placed under unauthorized or extreme forms of surveillance or observation that interfere with any reasonable expectation of privacy a student may have pursuant to campus policies or practices.[37]

Avoid a malfeasance claim by preventing willful blindness as to discoverable facts on the part of any entity conducting a misconduct investigation. The validity of the investigation is eroded where there is a high probability that facts exist regarding the alleged misconduct and the investigation takes deliberate action to avoid learning or discovering those facts.[38] Such action will cause the investigation to be characterized as nothing more than a mere "cover-up" or an effort to hide the truth, and should simply be discouraged. Student misconduct investigations will frequently reveal unpleasant truths about our students, our faculty, our colleagues, and yes, our institutions. People are imperfect and so are colleges and universities. The value of the internal investigation process is that it can provide a second chance for correction and renewal.

Student misconduct investigations begin with the best intentions. They aim to distinguish what is true from what is not and to ensure that all students are treated fairly and in a manner consistent with student conduct policies and procedures. However, these internal investigations are not ad hoc but are conducted within an institutional and legal framework shaped by the concerns and interests of congressional representatives as well as the programmatic priorities shared by student affairs administrators, faculty, and executive decision-makers at every level of the institution. The prudent student misconduct investigation is not elusive but can be achieved with a concerted effort that boldly pursues the *charge* of an investigation through the work of skilled higher education professionals.

Part II

The Student Misconduct Investigation

Chapter 3

Fundamentals

- -

Professor Ted Wright has taught world history at Utah College for dozens of semesters. At the end of each term it is his practice to review his learning objectives and visit with students regarding their grades or performance in the course if they request it. Following the recent spring semester, Professor Wright received an email from a student requesting an appointment to discuss her final grade. Because Professor Wright only had a listing of grades according to anonymous-grading numbers, he asked the registrar to provide the student's grade for the course in advance of their meeting.

After reviewing the student's grade, Professor Wright discovered that the grade assigned to the student did not match her anonymous-grading number. In fact, a detailed assessment of the grades for all the students in the history course revealed that multiple grades in the course had been altered. In an investigation that involved the academic affairs office, registrar, and information technology department, the College determined that two students had breached the computer system on campus to change their grades and the grades of other students.

Utah College has a computer usage policy that makes clear that students may be disciplined for improper conduct regarding the institution's computing hardware and software systems. The investigation was complicated because it involved multiple divisions within the College—namely, academic affairs (faculty), student affairs (registrar's office and student discipline), and administration (information technology and campus police). Although the College's investigation was fairly broad in scope and subject matter, it uncovered sufficient evidence to expel the students involved for violating the student honor code and academic misconduct. The next challenge is to determine if the investigation revealed breaches in the institution's computing systems that need to be resolved to prevent such a manipulation of data in the future.[1]

- - - - - - - - - -

Whether a student misconduct investigation is conducted by campus officials or with the help of an outside consultant, there will be a variety of persons engaged in the process. Depending on the seriousness of the alleged wrongdoing or misconduct, an administrator or a core group of administrators should be involved in making the decision to initiate the investigation and to determine what immediate steps should be taken to mitigate any harm or prevent any recurrence of misconduct. Furthermore, regardless of the scope or complexity of the disputed conduct, there are a series of fundamental steps that must be managed for an investigation to succeed. Administrators should

- establish the subject and focus of the investigation,
- select the appropriate investigator, and
- construct a proposed timeframe and strategy to move the investigation forward.

As previously noted, no two investigations are the same, but there are many common aspects that may impact the ultimate credibility of an inquiry. What procedures will be used to gather, share, and secure noteworthy information and evidence? What intervening steps will be taken to assure witnesses, the victim, and others who may have been victimized in some way by the alleged misconduct that there will not be any recurrence or retaliation? Colleges and universities should anticipate that their action and investigation efforts will be subject to scrutiny from external sources (parents, regulators, the media, the courts, legislators, etc.) and should be prepared to offer cogent responses that reflect transparency and thorough review.

The hypothetical Utah College grading scandal described above could happen at almost any college across the country. Any investigation would require similar basic steps as described. This chapter considers the significance these topics have on student misconduct internal investigations and provides helpful considerations for colleges and universities.

Authority, Accountability, and Charge of the Internal Investigation

Colleges, universities, and community colleges share a commitment to developing and implementing academic programs that are driven by the institution's mission. These institutions also face the common challenge of resolving student misconduct disputes by relying on investigation processes to identify relevant facts, assess the credibility of witnesses, and clarify the sequence of events to determine the need for disciplinary or remedial action. For public and private institutions of higher education, managing the typical challenges and unforeseeable mishaps that can confront a student's matriculation through his or her academic program is no small matter. At the very outset, there should be absolute clarity regarding under what *authority* the investigation is proceeding. Whether the authority originates from the student code of conduct, general campus safety rules, regulations that apply to students residing in campus residential facilities, or other college and university policies, it is critical that the investigation be authorized based on the institution's policies or sound student affairs protocols and practices.

The inability to demonstrate well-grounded authority for an investigation may expose an institution to claims that the investigation is arbitrary and capricious, or designed to target certain students for improper reasons. However, a student's pursuit of his or her educational, social, and other developmental goals through an academic institution cannot be jeopardized by unchecked scholastic or behavioral misconduct that disrupts the educational community. Colleges and universities are required to operate within a regulatory environment that flows from federal and state law, but institutions of higher education also have the inherent authority to ensure that student misconduct does not frustrate the academic process or undermine the institution's educational mission.[2]

It is also vital that *accountability* for the investigation be vested in an unambiguous institutional office or administrative unit.[3] However, colleges and universities are loosely coupled, decentralized organizations. Establishing clear lines of accountability for a student misconduct investigation can be complicated. For example, if a student-athlete is involved in some alleged misconduct, accountability for the investigation may rest with the athletic director and dean of students or may be collectively shared by multiple parties. In the case of a student involved in an online cheating scandal, accountability for the investigation may reside with the academic dean or department head with support provided by the information and technology department or campus police department.[4] In the event the matter under investigation results in litigation, issues regarding accountability can become an important subject of inquiry during the discovery process.

Conflicting statements about who is or is not accountable for certain phases of the investigation may raise suspicions about the fairness or adequacy of the investigation and any responsive action that seeks to rely on the investigation's findings of facts and conclusions. Further, to the extent campus officials are compelled to appear at depositions, any conflicting testimony provided that demonstrates material inconsistencies can undermine the validity of the investigation.

Once authorization and accountability for the investigation are considered and established, the *charge of the investigation* should be articulated prior to commencing the work. This can include drafting internal memoranda or documents that express the purpose and objectives of the investigation. When the institution decides to utilize legal counsel to conduct the student misconduct probe because litigation is anticipated, consideration should be given to invoking the attorney-client privilege and work-product doctrine in the document outlining the charge of the investigation (see chapter 5). This may be accomplished by stating the need for confidentiality and the involvement of the institution's attorney in the investigation process for the purpose of providing legal advice and counsel. The charge of the investigation may include a brief description of the events that have triggered the need for the inquiry and what is initially known about the chronology of relevant events and perceived important facts. The charge of the investigation may also include a plausible target date for completion of the work with the caveat that this date may be modified as needed.

Selecting the Investigator or Investigation Team

While it may be presumed that the selection of the internal investigator suggests the selection of a single investigator, the scope of some inquiries may require multiple investigators. In some disciplinary matters, colleges and universities have recognized various investigation models such as *the traditional model*, which includes an independent investigation with a separate hearing and appeals process; *the hybrid model,* which may include a single investigator who makes recommendations to a panel of decision-makers; or *the single investigator model,* wherein one individual conducts the investigation, interviews witnesses, makes credibility determinations, and renders findings, usually in a written report.[5] The public outcry or media attention that may accompany the need for an internal student misconduct investigation may also influence whether the institution decides to utilize one employee (or outside consultant) or an investigative team/consulting firm to conduct the investigation. Another option is to select a high-profile law firm or individual such as a former judge or public official to lead the investigation because people with this type of background not only have tremendous experience but also frequently have "name recognition" and credibility and perceived objectivity. While the investigator's professionalism and credibility are important, notoriety or popularity are secondary considerations, at best. Of course, factors such as the cost and timeliness may influence the investigation, so it is wise for colleges and universities to plan in advance of a crisis how investigators may be selected and retained.

Regardless of how the team is formulated, as a general matter, there is value in retaining an investigation team or an investigator that functions with the aid of support personnel during the inquiry process. The range of tasks that can flow from a student misconduct investigation can include managing multiple interviews where witnesses are available at conflicting times; having limited access to documents or evidence; as well as working around holidays and institutional closures, breaks, and periods of time outside the academic year that are not easily modified. However, the costs related to the internal investigation must be balanced against the increased efficiencies that are gained by retaining a team to guide the investigation rather than relying on one individual. Also, there may be good reason not to rely on a single investigator to conduct the entire disciplinary process related to due process challenges that may contend that an investigator was biased or lacked impartiality. Thus, the selection of the investigator or the investigation model should be taken seriously.

Higher education decision-makers selecting an investigator(s) should also ask key questions as they make their choice:

Which is better? An internal investigator or an external one? The individual selected to conduct the investigation should possess, or quickly develop, a thorough understanding of the institution's policies and procedures and should have a solid appreciation for the role the institution's student affairs practices have on the investigation process. Because of the lifelong impact campus experiences can have on students who are involved in misconduct disputes, restorative opportunities that surface during the investigation process must be taken advantage of as "teachable moments." For this reason, internal investigators may be advantageous because they have experience in student development and a natural connection to the institution. In all likelihood, they also have familiarity with helping students through difficult circumstances.

On the other hand, external investigators may have a similar skill set developed through strong ties within the higher education community that demonstrate a familiarity and sensitivity to student affairs as well as the institution's mission and values.

Is it imperative that the investigator have legal training? Yes, however he or she doesn't necessarily need to be an attorney. The investigator should have a broad understanding of the legal implications that may result from student misconduct or behavior and the ability to identify the legal and ethical obligations upon which the institution may have to act. Individuals with the requisite legal training may be licensed attorneys or non-lawyers with the educational background and credentials necessary to lead the investigation and identify legal and compliance concerns.

How important is the credibility of the investigator or team? Although one of the key functions of an internal investigation is to gather information and substantiate allegations with verifiable facts, it should also be hoped that the investigation will result in a final resolution that is perceived as fair. The selection of an unbiased, objective-minded investigator or team of investigation professionals will bolster the value of the investigation and the meaning of the investigative results. Investigators should be fair, impartial, and neutral fact finders.

When an investigator lacks credibility, the inquiry process may be viewed as nothing more than an exercise designed to affirm a predetermined outcome. Moreover, selecting an investigator who lacks credibility may be especially problematic if the institution's response and investigation of student misconduct becomes a triable legal issue before a judge or jury. Higher education experience and credentials are important considerations to weigh when selecting an investigator but credibility is also a vital concern.

Does the investigator have the right temperament for the job? For students raising complaints, students accused of misconduct, and witnesses who may have direct information about an alleged incident, interaction with the investigator will be critical. Although familiarity with the institution and legal knowledge are both necessary skills for an investigator, he or she must also have the proper temperament to manage these interviews and related contact. Student misconduct matters can have tremendous consequences for students in the here and now and also in their future. Given these realities, the investigator (or the investigative team) must be able to strike the proper tone with all parties during the investigative proceedings.

An investigator should project a calm and confident demeanor. In the process of the inquiry, he or she should be capable of de-escalating the customary tension and anxiety associated with any student misconduct investigation. An unruffled investigator is more likely to be successful at encouraging parties to the investigation and other witnesses to be forthcoming during the investigation process.

The Scope and Complexity of the Internal Investigation

As institutional officials contemplate whether to conduct an internal investigation, some thought should be given to the scope and complexity of the undertaking and managing any potential negative impact the investigation may have on student organizations, departments, personnel, and campus climate within the institution. The availability of students, faculty, or staff with personal information or who may have witnessed the incident should be determined as early as possible. Also, determining the number of people who may need to be interviewed will provide some insight into the breadth of the investigation. For example, a group of one to five persons to interview will be less demanding to reach than a group of fifteen to twenty people.

A practical approach to shaping investigation interviews might include classifying the people involved into categories:

- the *immediate* parties involved,
- people who *must* be interviewed, and
- people who *may* have relevant information.

Immediate parties will include the complainant and the student(s) accused of wrongdoing. People in the *must* category will include students or others identified by the complainant or the accused with relevant information, people who may have been within proximity of the incident, or people who are suspected of possessing verifiable information regarding the alleged student misconduct incident. People in the *may* category include students or institutional staff and faculty who might be familiar with the misconduct but have not been directly implicated in the matter. Persons in this category should be interviewed at the discretion of the investigator.

The scope and complexity of the internal investigation can also be influenced by which campus department or unit has a nexus with the alleged student misconduct incident. While

providing an exhaustive list of potential on-campus departments is difficult, the following offers some perspective on the
diverse array of areas that can serve as the backdrop for student
misconduct:

Athletic Department and the NCAA. Student-athletes are like
traditional students in some ways—that is, they have the
same academic hurdles to jump as students who do not
perform in athletic competition. However, at many schools
student-athletes are a unique segment of the student population and are exposed to certain relationships and opportunities that can heighten scrutiny. In some cases, student-athletes
possess a celebrity status and are known not only on their
campus but in the world of sports. Investigations involving
student-athletes may also involve the NCAA (the National
Collegiate Athletic Association)—further complicating
proceedings and inviting more public scrutiny. Incidents
involving admission and recruitment violations, academic
integrity, improper receipt of gifts, and allegations of assault or
other misconduct are just a few of the areas that can require
internal investigations of student-athletes.

*Office of International Programs and Education-Related Travel
Abroad.* Many colleges and universities have aggressively
sought to develop study-abroad programs, student exchange
programs, and other international ventures that take US
students to countries around the world. Institutions should
be prepared to gather data, collect information, and investigate
conduct incidents that happen abroad when students are
participating in academic programs on foreign soil. This will
include recognition of legal restrictions that may be controlling in foreign countries and limit investigation efforts
traditionally applied in the US.[6]

As an administrative matter, colleges and universities that
practice robust exchange programs are well advised to assess
the likely complexity of student misconduct investigations as a

preemptive action to determine whether specialized expertise is needed to conduct an investigation or evaluate evidence relative to the institution's programs. For example, for institutions that participate heavily in international programs, it would be prudent to have orientation programs for students and faculty outlining the continuing authority of campus policies and US law, as well as to spell out legal obligations that will apply in the host country where students will be visiting. Also, institutions should be prepared to deploy a "quick response team" in the event of an incident, capable of traveling to satellite campuses around the world, assessing the significance of any alleged mishap, and providing student support as needed. Protocols should be developed to identify legal counsel or other professionals on site (in country) who may be able to advocate for the institution in the best interests of students. This may also be more challenging depending on geographic location and/or language barriers. Hence, a student misconduct incident in Canada may be less demanding than an incident involving students in Vietnam.

Student Health Centers. Colleges and universities offer a variety of services to students in addition to health care through student health centers. To the extent an internal investigation is directed to a student's interaction with the student health center, institutional officials should understand that state and federal law limits an investigator's access to a student's personal health information. The Health Insurance Portability and Accountability Act of 1996 (HIPAA) and the Family Educational Rights and Privacy Act (FERPA) may prohibit disclosure of student health information for privacy reasons. However, under some circumstances, such as where a student presents a danger to herself/himself or others, the institution acting in good faith may have a legitimate basis to release health information under the guidance and advice of legal counsel.

Office of Career Services/Off-Campus Placements. In addition to participating in traditional classroom instruction, students completing degree programs often have the opportunity to expand their learning by taking part in practical experiences in professional and practitioner settings. However, participation in an off-campus externship program does not relieve students of their obligation to abide by their home institution's student conduct rules and regulations. When student misconduct investigations are required at placement locations, academic units should have protocols or, perhaps, a memorandum of understanding with institutional partners to cooperate with necessary investigations.

For example, assume a student is enrolled in a student-teaching field placement to complete an education degree program but is dismissed from the field placement for unspecified reasons. Because of the impact on a student's degree requirements some level of investigation may be required to determine what action is necessary. Was the student's removal from the field placement appropriate? What was the nature of the student's misconduct? These questions and others will be easier to explore with a coherent plan in place to investigate student activities at off-campus locations.

Regardless of the numerous circumstances that trigger the need for a substantive investigation, understanding the *scope* and *complexity* of the matter are fundamental considerations. Scope and complexity of an investigation may require the investigator or the investigation team to have skills or competencies regarding social media, access to support personnel who are bilingual, or familiarity with medical terminology or the effects of certain medication on behavior. While it is difficult to prepare an exhaustive list of the kinds of expertise that may be needed in any particular student misconduct investigation, it is critical that the investigation has the capacity to probe and scrutinize a range of issues that may surface during the investigation process.

Purpose, Subject Matter, and Outcomes

With the authority and charge of the investigation well defined, it may appear redundant to make additional comments about the purpose or subject matter of the internal investigation. However, a fundamental tenet of an internal investigation includes a disciplined focus on the subject matter. Focus on the purpose and subject matter of the investigation can be difficult to maintain because during the course of an investigation issues, problems, and matters not included in the charge or scope of the investigation can surface. For example, an investigation that is initially commenced to determine whether a student's residence hall room was properly searched consistent with campus safety policies respecting a student's rights under the Fourth Amendment could unnecessarily drift into an audit of training programs provided for Resident Assistants and Residence Hall Directors. This is not to minimize the importance of the range of issues that may be uncovered during an investigation but there is value in the statement offered by author Stephen Covey: "The main thing is to keep the main thing the main thing."[7] Internal investigations are effective when driven by a focused purpose. An unguided investigation that rambles indefinitely and is inclined to be sidetracked by annoying institutional inefficiencies may be interesting but, in the end, does not provide a purposeful review of the matter in question.

An internal investigation that avoids the temptation to drift and remains focused on its purpose will have the best chance of producing meaningful outcomes. Meaningful outcomes may include a transparent description of the events as told and understood by witnesses and those involved, supported by materially relevant information and facts that have been verified, as well as a listing of alleged facts and bits and pieces of information that cannot be corroborated at the time the investigation is brought to a close. Of course, the quest for certainty in every detail will always be in high demand. But, rarely do investigations have access to unlimited resources or function without some time constraints. For student affairs administrators, the time constraints could simply be that the semester is nearing an end, the exam period is underway, or a holiday period has begun and students and faculty may have less availability.

Where definitive answers cannot be obtained, an internal investigation that provides meaningful information for academic and student services decision-makers can still be valuable. The meaningful outcomes can aid administrators in determining what immediate remedial action is necessary, how to eliminate potential threats, and where to concentrate institutional resources. For instance, if hostilities have emerged that involve students on campus, an investigation that does not result in the identification of specific individuals may still be meaningful if the investigation can determine that those potentially involved are confined to a small set or if certain groups are determined to be uninvolved in the hostility.

The Reporting Chain

Any number of people will have a role to play during the course of an internal investigation and the subsequent remedial action. As the number of persons involved in the investigation expands, so will the volume of voices and commentary offered. While there may be little reason to suspect bad faith from any institutional representative, there are good reasons to have an unambiguous reporting chain. Investigators and campus officials need to communicate during an investigation frequently to address logistics questions, receive status reports and updates, or simply to grant access to documents, people, and other evidence. While many of these tasks may include routine matters that do not require any special skill set, it is important for mundane assignments like scheduling conference rooms, checking calendars, and making copies of documents get done efficiently and effectively.

On the other end of the spectrum, the investigators and campus officials should have a working knowledge of the chain of command to discuss and resolve critical and sensitive issues that will arise during the investigation. This also should include clarification regarding whether and how the lead or principal investigator should share crucial concerns with the university's general counsel, vice president for student affairs, or an academic dean. Do these people have confidential assistants who can relay questions or information? How can key players be reached on weekends or outside of normal business hours?

Another key issue to clarify is which modes of communication are acceptable. The use of cellphones, text messaging, video conferencing, and email should not simply be presumed but deserves some acknowledgment from the participating parties as an agreeable method through which to communicate and share information. This can be an important consideration if the investigation becomes an issue in litigation where telephone records and other electronic communications are sought through discovery requests.

It is critical to understand the impact an internal investigation regarding student misconduct, or alleged misconduct, can have on a campus community. The rumor mill is forever thirsty for news of any kind of hot gossip, for sure. Having a clear, secure reporting chain staffed by responsible people can go a long way to minimizing information breaches or leaks that do nothing more than fuel campus unrest. These handlers or persons in the reporting chain between the investigator or investigation team and institutional decision-makers need not be numerous but should have a broad store of institutional knowledge and proven problem-solving capabilities.

Also, persons within the reporting chain should understand the importance of handling confidential information. Because people in the reporting chain may have access to sensitive information, and may be facilitating the exchange of documents and data relevant to the investigation, they will be in a position to breach the integrity of the investigation by sharing what they know with others who do not have a *bona fide* need to know. Furthermore, people who may have been involved in an investigation that is subsequently the subject of a lawsuit may be called upon to testify or answer questions during a deposition under oath about their observations during the investigation process. It is worth stating that the testimony of these people may be protected under the attorney-client privilege and they may be barred from making any disclosures. However, for these reasons, persons in the reporting chain should have noteworthy credibility because their actions may be subject to review and scrutiny by various interested parties.

Timing

Student behavior can trend in certain directions during the academic year, but it is far from predictable on a regular basis. For instance, toward the end of an academic semester or quarter, with the exam period looming, stress and anxiety can be elevated because students are preparing for tests or meeting deadlines for various projects. At the beginning of a semester students may have more opportunity to party. In other words, student behavior may be influenced by timing. That said, student misconduct can happen at almost any time, without warning, and when it does, a resulting internal investigation may face plenty of hurdles of its own related to timely *scheduling*. The typical academic calendar has a reasonable share of holidays, breaks, and other recognized periods of time that can make scheduling the witness interviews challenging. For example, for an internal investigation that is commenced in November or December, the Thanksgiving holiday, Christmas holiday, or other academic break can delay the progress of an investigation by weeks or even months. Further, when the investigation is dependent on interviewing or taking statements from faculty or other employees, the unavailability of these people for reasons related to personal leave, vacation, sabbatical, or other absences can also delay an investigation.

Investigators and those responsible for an internal investigation should appreciate that "delay is an enemy" of the prompt, responsive investigation. Students accused of wrongdoing or those who may have witnessed misconduct should give statements while their memories are fresh. Acting in cooperation with legal counsel, student affairs administrators and investigators may consider asking witnesses to provide a written statement to capture their recollection of certain events. Such written statements may be produced as affidavits or declarations that are provided under oath, thereby attesting to the truthfulness of the statements.

In order to ensure that timing concerns do not unduly interfere with the investigation, a fundamentally sound tactic is to identify the logistical or scheduling issues that may interfere with access to students and key staff as early as possible and take steps to mitigate the impact of any challenges that might delay the investigation. For example, offer to interview students before holiday breaks, consider interviewing witnesses by Skype or other means of electronic communication, or offer to travel to the location convenient for the witnesses to avoid substantial delays.[8] Although the timeframe for the investigation should remain flexible, some conservative projection should be made as to when the investigation will begin and end. But such timeframe expectations always must be subordinate to the objective pursuit of relevant, material information regarding the charge of the investigation.

Structuring the Investigation Plan

A final fundamental component of the internal investigation that merits consideration is the formation of an investigation plan that galvanizes the various components of the investigation process. The investigation plan should be viewed as a script or playbook that describes the framework and certain details regarding the investigation. At a minimum, the investigation plan should clarify the following issues:

- the charge of the investigation;
- the scope of the investigation and the student misconduct allegations under review;
- a preliminary witness list that distinguishes complainant and accused from other witnesses who may be interviewed. The investigation plan may also indicate the likely order in which witnesses may be interviewed;
- a proposed timeline for the execution and completion of the investigation; and
- whether the internal investigation is a confidential inquiry commenced in anticipation of litigation and invoked by the institution's legal counsel under which the attorney-client privilege and/or the work-product doctrine are applicable.

Also, the investigation plan should account for the various legal and policy nuances that must be observed for students and employees who may be implicated as complainants, alleged perpetrators, or witnesses during the investigation. For instance, a student who comes forward claiming that she has been a victim of sexual violence will trigger an entirely different set of responses than a student who has been identified by a faculty member as allegedly engaging in plagiarism. Under federal law, the institution's Title IX Coordinator will be involved in a sexual misconduct incident, persons designated as "responsible employees" will have reporting obligations, and federal agencies and local law enforcement may commence a separate inquiry as well. By comparison, an investigation regarding academic integrity due to an act of plagiarism, while a serious act of misconduct, poses a threat to the academic community that is different in nature and gravity than an incident involving sexual violence.

When students and faculty or other university employees are involved in a student misconduct incident, the institution's human resources personnel should be consulted to ensure that policies regarding employees are not violated. An important precaution may include advising employees that the institution's nondiscrimination policies prohibit any retaliatory action against employees and others who come forward with information regarding student misconduct. Where employees are represented by a union, employee protections are often expressed in the collective bargaining agreement (CBA) and should also receive careful attention during the investigation process.

Practical Considerations

Strive to promote institutional harmony by observing the following guidelines:

Students should never be discouraged from reporting misconduct. False allegations, reports that are not made in good faith, are, at the very least, improper and can themselves be a basis for disciplinary action where there is an intent to deceive or mislead others. However, students should not be left to take matters into their own hands, or forced to endure circumstances that interfere with their educational opportunities or unfairly limit the rights and privileges that are ordinarily available to students. Institutions should provide students with multiple avenues to report various forms of on- and off-campus misconduct and be prepared to offer support services.
Media disclosures should be truthful and accurate. Student misconduct incidents rarely merit a press release or press conference. But when an internal investigation dictates that the institution issue a response to the campus community or the public at-large, the institution's messaging should be thoughtful, impartial, and mindful of privacy concerns. Statements offered should be reviewed by persons experienced

with the media and crisis management, and should not be overly detailed. Nor should they release confidential information (see chapter 4 for a discussion of communications with the press and the media).

The investigation process should be objective, fair, and consistent with previous practices. Higher education constantly observes the arrival, matriculation, and departure of students through degree programs to graduation, etc. It's a natural process that is intended to happen. Faculty and staff also come and go for reasons related to their career development and other personal objectives. While the student body and human resources that comprise our institutions of higher education will change over time, the policies and practices that drive student misconduct investigations cannot fluctuate with personnel changes. For students and staff, the equitable campus investigation must endure through an ongoing commitment to educate the student community and train academic and student affairs personnel to perform the investigation function at a high level. *Investigators should be aware of the effect of silos and decentralization.* Departments and units within a college or university may develop practices or informal procedures to manage student conflict. However, where these practices are inconsistent with campuswide policies and compliance requirements in different sectors of the campus, students may be subject to differential treatment. Avoid a fragmented approach to student affairs. Regular training across academic units, and especially to particular areas such as intercollegiate athletics and international programs, should be conducted to share baseline fundamentals (dare I say "best practices") that should permeate any student misconduct inquiry. Of course, students in the medical school will be subject to different oversight than a student-athlete who is a member of the women's basketball team. But the institution should not be at the mercy of its programmatic and academic diversification.

To summarize, the internal investigation can and should be an effective tool for the institution to resolve and manage student misconduct incidents. The capacity for campus decision-makers to get reliable information quickly enhances the institution's ability to minimize the harm that may flow from adverse behavior. However, internal investigations cannot run the risk of being reckless and ill conceived. To act in this way places our students in jeopardy.

Chapter 4

Tactics

Cellphones, PDAs, tablets, and other electronic computing devices that have the capacity to capture video and audio recordings have proven to be a tremendous evidentiary resource. Consider the alleged sexual assault of Dana South, a freshman at Metropolitan College (MC), by two male students. Dana, a stereotypical freshman, is 19 years old and excited about college, although she has not yet settled on an academic major. Most of all, Dana has been thrilled to be on her own and is enjoying the social freedoms of college life.

Dana had some modest dating experience in high school but most of her encounters ended in disappointment and broken friendships at best. During Dana's first semester on campus, she lived in student housing and made friends easily with several students in the female-only wing of her residence hall. However, Dana lived for the weekend. On Friday and Saturday nights she looked forward to going to the nearby party spot, popularly referred to as "the Hill." The Hill is a two-block area comprised of bars, restaurants, and lots of opportunities for students to dance, hear live music, and, for those 18 years old or older, to consume lots of alcohol. The Hill is a popular meet-and-greet spot for students where the hook-up culture thrives in a party atmosphere.

On the Saturday night in question, Dana met Robert Jones and Lee Haley, both MC undergraduate students as well. The three hit it off right away. Robert and Lee took turns dancing with Dana and after each dance the guys insisted on buying another round of drinks. After consuming drinks that included beer, vodka, whisky, and rum, Dana pulled out her cellphone and started taking pictures. Robert and Lee also took pictures with their cellphones and even some video.

As the night grew late, the three began walking back to campus. According to Dana, Robert and Lee took her cellphone and refused to return it. Apparently, Dana followed the two male students to their dormitory in an effort to retrieve her cellphone, but was lured into a men's bathroom where she was sexually assaulted by Robert and Lee. Dana described the incident as a brutal rape where the two male students took turns sexually assaulting her while the other held her down despite her cries for help and pleas that the forcible sexual contact stop. When it did stop, Dana said she was left in the bathroom of the men's dormitory alone and somehow managed to return to her residence hall.

The next morning Dana reported the incident to campus authorities and the local police, which triggered an investigation. Robert and Lee faced not just dismissal from MC but jail time if convicted of assaulting Dana. The incident got tremendous media attention. Both Robert and Lee explained to the police and campus investigators that they did have sex with Dana but that it was consensual. Dana's allegations were viewed as credible based on eyewitness accounts that supported her claims that her cellphone was taken by Robert or Lee, and that she may have been lured to their dormitory to retrieve it.

However, just before the close of the campus investigation (and news that the local prosecutor intended to pursue rape charges against the male students) new evidence emerged. Robert and Lee provided a video recording the sexual encounter with Dana that included audio taken with Lee's cellphone. The video shows that Dana, Robert, and Lee engaged in consensual sex. The video was shown to Dana, who did not dispute its depiction of the incident. The charges against Robert and Lee were dropped, and MC is considering disciplinary action against Dana for making false claims.[1]

Just because there is smoke does not mean that an actual fire is underway. The commencement of a student misconduct investigation does not mean that there has been student misconduct. The conduct of Robert and Lee may have been far from honorable, to say the least, but the investigation process has to be objective, free of preconceived findings or outcomes. This chapter explores the process of identifying witnesses, conducting witness interviews, assessing credibility, collecting documents, and the impact these activities have on revealing facts and verifying what is and is not true. In addition to providing some guidelines for communicating with the media, I hope to make clear the value of the all-important "pause"—often provided by the internal investigation—in avoiding a haphazard rush to judgment.

Once the scope and structure for conducting the investigation are established (see chapter 3), the detailed work of collecting information, data, and evidence that verifies misconduct allegations or indicates that there is insufficient information to support an alleged student misconduct charge should begin without delay and with a full understanding of an investigation's time objectives. Generally, the time objectives that will influence an internal investigation will face two important constraints: it is often not easy to predict the expected length of an investigation, and the longer the investigation takes the more likely it is that documentation could be lost or corrupted.

The first time objective is to commence the student misconduct investigation as soon as possible after the alleged incident. The swift commencement is important because relevant information, which can include photographs, video or audio recordings, as well as digital and electronic communication, may emerge from numerous sources. Delays in starting the investigation can impact the ability of investigators to capture documents, witness statements, and other evidence that can fade or be lost over the passage of time. Regardless of the sources, the tactics applied to gathering information relevant to the investigation should focus on timeliness, authenticity, and ensuring that information collected during the investigation is maintained in its original condition, free from tampering or manipulation.[2] The second time objective involves identifying a plausible completion date or timeframe as established by campus officials to bring closure to an internal investigation. The problem here is that a projected completion date for an internal investigation may not be easy to determine, and may, to a large degree, be driven by the complexity of the alleged misconduct.

In the interest of due process, transparency, and advising students of disciplinary policies and procedures triggered by student misconduct, many colleges and universities choose to notify students of the investigatory procedures through the student handbook, the student code of conduct, or other student affairs materials. However, internal investigations are not rigid or inflexible proceedings and may deviate from guidelines or language set forth in student handbooks without unduly trammeling due process interests.[3]

Students involved in the investigation process and related disciplinary proceedings do not forfeit their student status because they may be implicated in a student misconduct matter. While expulsion, suspension, or some form of temporary or permanent dismissal may be available options to remove from campus students who pose a threat to themselves or others, the investigation should aid the institution in determining whether such action is justified or necessary.

The outcome and consequences of campus disciplinary proceedings may lead some of the students involved to eventually become litigants. Students can become plaintiffs in a civil action or defendants in a criminal prosecution. Student affairs professionals, university counsel, and other academic administrators should not overlook a witness's student status, especially where the internal investigation authorized by the college or university may be viewed as simply a prelude to civil litigation, which is an inherently adversarial process. To that end, student witnesses should be encouraged to speak freely during interviews, and any questioning tactics that resemble coercion or that place student witnesses under duress should be avoided at all times. Preparing to interview a student witness with input from university legal advisors may be a useful balance between student affairs objectives that are concerned with supportive outreach to a student and the need to remain mindful that a student may subsequently bring legal claims against the institution.

As for documents, the content and meaning of substantive materials may be self-evident in most cases, but documents must be carefully examined and reviewed to verify their authenticity. Moreover, every effort should be made to ensure that the chain of custody for documents recovered as a part of the investigation is sustainable to prevent loss, destruction, or corruption.

Identifying Witnesses

Information helpful to a student misconduct internal investigation can emerge through statements or observations from persons across the entire campus. Student witnesses may be best positioned to offer insight regarding a particular incident due to proximity or relationship with parties to the incident. In addition to students, faculty members and university employees who serve as support staff, counselors, athletic coaches, or in a range of other positions within the institution can have important information to share. However, student witnesses may be managed differently from university employees, especially in cases where employees are granted certain rights or protections through contractual agreements, are subject to rules and regulations spelled out in employee handbooks, or are affected by obligations that limit the disclosure of personnel information.

Nonetheless, even where employees are involved in student misconduct investigations, student witnesses indeed will need to be advised, on some limited level, why the employees are being interviewed without violating the employee's rights.[4]

For parties to alleged incidents of sexual violence or sexual assault in violation of Title IX, the institution must advise the complainants and alleged perpetrators that a prompt investigation will be undertaken, interim measures like counseling services will be made available, and periodic updates on the status of the investigation will follow. In all cases, investigations must offer student complainants, alleged perpetrators, and other witnesses an equal opportunity to offer relevant evidence to the investigation.

The identification of witnesses with personal information regarding an act of student misconduct will be dependent on a timely effort to collect information about the scene of the alleged student misconduct incident, thereby providing investigators with a viable list of sources and potential witnesses. Useful information may include email messages, video recordings, classroom lists, or directory information that identifies students. Electronic or digital information transmitted or communicated using the institution's computing hardware, servers, or other modes of electronic communication made available by the college or university should be explored during the data collection process. Students (and employees as a human resources matter) should be advised that the institution reserves the right to examine electronic communication pursuant to campus policies.

However, the student complainant and the accused student or perpetrator themselves may be the most productive sources from which to identify student witnesses with reliable information. College and university orientation programs and student handbooks should encourage students to come forward with information pertaining to misconduct on campus, and it should be made clear that participating in a student misconduct investigation will not subject a student to discrimination or retaliation.

While it is a practical necessity to interview the complainant, the accused, and other witnesses who may have relevant information, not all institutions have defined policies and practices that trigger this approach. Private colleges and universities may have different procedures in place. In many situations, student misconduct incidents can be resolved quickly or the facts can be easily understood without an extensive inquiry for various reasons. Students involved in misconduct may simply admit their wrongdoing when approached about a particular incident. Or, indisputable evidence may be available, such as a video recording, that identifies a student's whereabouts and participation in an incident. For those matters where the quick and easy resolution is not available, institutions of higher education, both public and private, should have policies and practices in place that allow for robust investigation processes but do not require such action in every case. Put another way, campus administrators must have discretion regarding the investigation process.

In *Schaer v. Brandeis University*, the court considered the university investigation regarding a student disciplinary matter that involved unwelcome sexual activity. Examining the private university's policies, the court determined that the university's handbook provision governing investigations of reported privacy violations was inapplicable to investigations regarding student misconduct. The handbook provision governing information gathered in connection with disciplinary proceedings did not require the university to take particular steps to obtain evidence from students or allow students to present evidence. Addressing the specific section from the university handbook, the court stated:

> Section 17 provides, in relevant part: "[T]he available facts shall be gathered from the [complainant] and a careful evaluation of these facts, as well as the credibility of the person reporting them, shall be made. If corroboration of the information presented is deemed necessary, further inquiry and investigation shall be undertaken."

Nothing in this section requires university officials to obtain an interview from the accused student, to seek evidence from the accused student, or to grant the accused student an opportunity to provide witnesses at the investigatory stage in the proceedings.[5]

In short, private institutions act pursuant to contract and can impose ample flexibility into investigation procedures. Institutional documents drafted by campus officials may outline rules, policies, and conduct codes that govern student disciplinary action. These documents can be scrutinized in a court of law but state and federal mandates often force public as well as private colleges and universities to maintain certain investigation protocols. For example, today Title IX demands a more standardized protocol for sexual assault investigations.[6] However, *Schaer v. Brandeis University* stands as a reminder that private institutions may act in a manner that is distinguishable from public colleges and universities.

Assessing Witness Credibility

The investigation process may be best served by the information provided by witnesses through interviews and any statements that might be offered in writing. Witnesses certainly can offer admissions to misconduct or undisputed statements that can be corroborated by supporting evidence and information. However, conflicting statements from various witnesses will likely emerge during an internal investigation that will force investigators to assess the credibility of witnesses. The critical question focuses on whether the witness has offered truthful statements. Determining whether a witness is credible is more of an art than a science. Among the factors that may be considered when determining credibility are the following: plausibility, demeanor, bias, and prior statements on record. These factors should be evaluated by observing the witness interviews in person.[7]

Plausibility refers to whether the testimony of a given witness may indeed be determined as consistent with the events and circumstances relevant to the investigation. Students and other persons interviewed during the course of a misconduct investigation should be expected to link their observations through a detailed recounting of the incident timeline. Direct observation of a witness's *demeanor* when providing testimony can influence investigators as well. Observing a witness's tone of voice, appearance, and general behavior during the interview may help investigators decide if a witness is lying or offering truthful statements during an interview. By comparison, determining that the witness may be *biased* often rests on less subjective information, such as evidence indicating that the witness and another party in the investigation had a relationship that could influence the witness's testimony. This might include not only personal relationships but organizational affiliations that students may maintain with official student organizations and other groups (for example, fraternities, sororities, intercollegiate athletics teams, political groups, etc.). Also, a witness's credibility can be undermined by showing that he or she has offered *prior inconsistent statements* or if there is a record that the witness has made conflicting statements. For students, especially graduate students pursuing degrees and credentials to enter professional fields that require a license, such as medicine or law, giving untruthful or knowingly misleading testimony can have career ramifications. Information that points to the likelihood that a witness is being untruthful can be tricky and far from simple. The rumor mill on college campuses can be as vast and unpredictable as that in any segment of American society. Therefore, speculation that a witness is lying should probably be tempered by determining what motive he or she may have to be untruthful.

Students can be a valuable source of information for an internal investigation and simply cannot be ignored or overlooked. But the investigation must take account of likely breaches in the student's credibility. No single factor can determine that a student lacks credibility. The investigation's fact-finding process must examine whether there are legitimate reasons to determine whether a student's rendition of the facts are believable, and if not, explain why. In this regard, an investigator's capacity to remain impartial and avoid being unduly influenced by emotional or prejudicial forces will be important. For example, assume a seemingly peaceful on-campus debate is sponsored by students affiliated with the "Black Lives Matter" movement, after which a heated exchange ensues in a campus parking lot between students who attended the event and other students who showed up to protest the event. Students are injured, there is lots of property damage, and tremendous pressure for the institution to take action. In this situation, emotions are running high, thus, the need for credible testimony from student witnesses could not be more imperative.

Interviewing Witnesses and Sequencing the Order of Interviews

The task of interviewing witnesses requires thoughtful preparation and planning. Anything less may result in missed opportunities to gain valuable insight regarding the circumstances related to the complaint, the parties involved, and whether evidence exists to substantiate a violation of campus rules or regulations. To prevent such mishaps, it's important to have a sound approach to each witness interview. This begins by developing a profile of each potential witness identified to be interviewed as part of the investigation. The *witness profile* should include information relevant to the investigation regarding the witness's involvement or connection to the alleged wrongdoing and/or parties to the incident. Such information may include confirming the student's identity, enrollment status, and whether he or she is in good standing at the university. Also, collecting what information is available that places a potential witness at the scene of the incident will be helpful in preparing for a witness interview. As the investigation moves forward, each witness profile should be further developed, supplemented, and amended as needed to ensure accuracy. The witness profile should serve as an important resource for investigators and campus decision-makers and provide a reasonable basis from which to become familiar with and distinguish witnesses from one another.

Furthermore, in preparation for each witness interview, an *interview outline* should be drafted to guide the investigator's questioning during the interview. It is not uncommon for a whirlwind of issues to surround student misconduct disputes, not to mention the campus disruption and inherent pressure placed on the investigation process to move quickly. However, when it comes to interviewing witnesses, expediency cannot take priority over thoroughness. First-time witness interviews are usually the investigator's best opportunity to get a clear picture of an individual's observations, when the witness's memory may be most reliable. Thus, it is critical that investigators meticulously question witnesses about all relevant issues and disputes within the scope of the investigation. Every interview should address the bullet items below:

- Confirm basic information about the witness—name and identity, enrollment status at the institution, contact information. For students, directory information may be available to confirm the basic identity of witnesses.
- Explain the purpose of the interview and reassure the witness that he or she will not be subjected to adverse action for participating in the investigation and sharing truthful information to the best of his or her recollection in good faith. In the case of a Title IX investigation, the institution's Title IX Coordinators or Sexual Assault Response Coordinator should be consulted regarding the clarification of rights, remedies, and protections available to complainants.

- Pose open-ended questions about matters which the witness has personal knowledge of—when events were observed, witness's whereabouts or location, witness's capacity or limitations relative to observations.
- Request a review of documents, photographs, recordings, electronic communications, and other things the witness has custody of related to observations.
- Explain the alleged violations of relevant rules, procedures, or regulations. Also, as appropriate, give the witness the opportunity to rebut, respond, or provide alternative explanations to alleged violations.
- Ask the witness to describe his or her activities before, during, and after the alleged student misconduct incident.
- Explore the identity of all persons the witness has knowledge of who played a role in the incident and determine the scope of their involvement.
- Conclude the interview with a final invitation for the witness to share additional information or clarify any previous remarks.
- Determine the witness's availability in the near future for follow-up questions and urge the witness to contact the investigator should the witness need to refresh his or her responses or for other reasons.

As the process of interviewing witnesses gets underway, the order or sequence in which witnesses are interviewed should not be left to chance. Interviewing the complainant or the person(s) that may have been victimized by the alleged student misconduct is often the best place to begin. Interviewing these individuals first will give the investigator an initial sense of the severity or pervasiveness of the alleged student misconduct and whether immediate remedial action is necessary to prevent the recurrence of the alleged wrongdoing or misconduct. Further, if a more particularized intervention is needed, such as medical care, counseling, or judicial action that may seek a protective order, interviewing the complainant and the alleged perpetrator at the early stages of the investigation will be invaluable.

Other witnesses should be interviewed according to availability and based upon an assessment of the witness's capacity to share relevant important information. As previously indicated, witnesses may include other students but can also emerge from the faculty, support staff, or vendors who may be on campus periodically. Before questioning institutional employees such as faculty or staff personnel, consult with university legal counsel and human resources administrators. College and university employees should be advised regarding their obligations to answer questions posed during an internal investigation.[8] Likewise, investigators should be prepared to handle employees' objections to answering questions based on academic freedom or other grounds.[9] Finally, witnesses should be advised that if they have questions following the interview or would like to supplement their responses to any questions, they should contact the investigator, or a member of the investigative team, directly. They should not contact other persons who did not participate in their interview.[10]

Fairness in Disclosures to Students and Other Witnesses

The term "ex parte" means "from one party" and refers to an action or proceeding wherein a judge or decision-maker confers with or discloses information only to one party without granting an opposing party an opportunity to respond or participate contemporaneously. In some circumstances, the ex parte presentation of evidence may be justified. For example, where it is necessary to protect the anonymity of student witnesses or the disclosure of highly confidential information is at issue. In the course of student misconduct investigations, however, ex parte investigative action that results in the collection and consideration of evidence germane to the student misconduct complaint can lead to an infringement of a student's due process rights and should be avoided. In *Univ. of Texas Med. Sch. at Hous-*

ton v. Than, a medical student was dismissed from a public university for academic dishonesty—allegedly cheating on a National Board of Medical Examiners (NBME) exam.[11] During the course of the disciplinary proceeding, the disciplinary hearing officer conducted an inspection of the testing room where the alleged cheating occurred. The court characterized the investigation of the testing room as follows:

> [T]he hearing officer personally examined the site where the test was conducted, accompanied only by Dr. McNeese [the academic administrator]. Than [student accused] asked to accompany them to the testing room, but the hearing officer refused. No contemporaneous record exists of what transpired during the hearing officer's inspection of the exam room. However, the hearing officer testified by deposition that on her visit to the test site she sat in four different chairs, representing the place occupied by Than, Mr. Chiang, the student from whom Than allegedly cheated, and the two proctors. In her report concluding that Than should be expelled, she lists as one of her findings that "I sat in the chair occupied by Mr. Than during the examination and could clearly see the paper from the examination chair occupied by Mr. Chiang." In determining Than's guilt, the hearing officer relied, at least in part, on the evidence she obtained while sitting in those chairs.[12]

The court determined that the medical student was entitled to a new hearing on the academic dishonesty charge because the hearing officer's decision to expel the student, at least in part, relied on evidence she obtained through an ex parte investigation to which the accused student was not afforded the opportunity to respond.[13] The student was not contemporaneously, or at any other moment, given the chance to rebut the hearing officer's interpretation or view of the test site seating arrangement or any other observations that may have been raised during the ex parte inspection of the testing room. In granting the student a new hearing, the court noted that the student's protected liberty interest in continuing his medical education and restoring his good name was substantial and that his due process rights were violated because he was *denied an opportunity to respond to or rebut evidence against him.*

Similar allegations were raised by two former University of Oregon student-athletes. The former basketball players, who were dismissed from the team in 2014 after being named in a police report regarding an alleged off-campus sexual assault, filed a civil lawsuit against the university alleging that the institution's investigation was biased and did not allow them to present witnesses. The critical question raised herein considers the plausibility of a due process violation because the investigation denied the student-athletes an opportunity to respond to or rebut evidence against them by not allowing the students to present witnesses.[14]

An internal investigation's dependence on productive, thorough witness interviews cannot be overstated, nor can the significance of a fair and impartial investigative process that respects a student's due process rights. A failure to capture the observations, impressions, or eyewitness accounts of the events and circumstances regarding student misconduct incidents substantially undermines the institution's ability to determine and implement corrective action. Therefore, student affairs professionals and other personnel responsible for conducting witness interviews should concentrate on the following:

Focus on facts. It is likely that a witness will have some degree of anxiety for any number of reasons or perhaps a witness may have some predetermined agenda that has motivated him or her to come forward. Regardless of the nervousness or motivation of witnesses, they should be given the opportunity to express themselves through answers to open-ended questions that explore the charge and scope of the investigation. The focus of the interview must be placed on gathering facts that should be distinguished from rumors, opinions, or other statements based on speculation.

Give priority to witnesses with personal knowledge. Statements, comments, and other matters discovered from a witness with personal knowledge should be given priority over information based on a witness's opinion or bare speculation. Personal knowledge is defined as knowledge acquired firsthand or from observation and is distinguished from a belief based on what another person has uttered or commented upon.[15] Personal knowledge does not refer to hearsay but rather knowledge acquired or perceived through an individual's own senses.[16] While any statements or information relevant to the incident under investigation may indeed deserve review and analysis, information offered from a witness with personal knowledge has more credibility and can be verified. Therefore, it is important to question a witness regarding the basis for his or her statements or observations and to discern how they came to learn matters related to the investigation. Where a witness speaks without personal knowledge, his or her statements will require confirmation from another source or be designated as unverifiable for purposes of the investigation.

Distinguish materially relevant information. The fairness and integrity of the internal investigation will remain a central concern for all parties during the investigation process, thereby placing the institution's reputation in the spotlight as well. For a college or university to avoid challenges to the investigation itself it is vital that the investigators concentrate on the collection of information that is material and relevant, differentiating that information from statements, documents, or other evidence that are speculative or argumentative.

Determining materiality can be difficult but ultimately involves a fact-specific inquiry that points to information that may lead investigators or decision-makers to reach verifiable findings regarding a student's alleged misconduct. The investigation will likely uncover numerous matters that may have some bearing on student academic or behavioral conduct as well as on the well-being of students and faculty across the campus. While these matters should not be ignored per se, the pursuit of relevant documents and material witness interviews should not be overpowered by the temptation to drift into matters that are not material and relevant to the charge of the internal investigation. Furthermore, investigators should anticipate the rise of ancillary matters during the investigation and be prepared to promptly delegate those matters to others.

*Encourage students to act in good faith.*While the preparation for witness interviews is important, ultimately, what a witness agrees to share also will be influenced by intangibles that require skill and sensitivity to navigate. The most important intangible may be the sense of relationship an individual has with the institution and how that comports with a witness's willingness to be forthcoming and act in good faith. Students can be truthful, blatantly dishonest, intentionally vague, or even noncompliant during an interview.[17] Whether a student chooses to cooperate and be helpful can be determined by the comfort level developed before, during, and after the witness interview. Matters regarding student conflict can stem from the demands to perform in curricular and extracurricular programs or the pressure that flows from the rigorous academic standards that permeate degree programs. In either case, the internal investigation process must account for these concerns and the impact they may have on student witnesses. In *Coster v. DuQuette,* a student charged with plagiarism, lying to her professor, and taking another student's examination paper from the professor's mailbox was found liable for conversion.[18] The university's investigation compared the writing styles, grammar, and references used by the examination papers at issue. However, it was the student's own testimony that would prove to be most incriminating. The student testified that she saved her final examination paper on the university computer system on a specific date. This was not credible when viewed in comparison to conflicting testimony offered by a communications and technology consultant, which showed that the student electronically submitted her paper almost a week later. Hence, the value of credible information provided from students in good faith cannot be overstated. In this case, the student's dishonesty was offset by expert testimony, however, in many situations the institution is left only with statements from witnesses where credibility is vital.

The Special Case of Collective Student Misconduct

In the summer of 2017 Harvard University rescinded admission offers to at least ten entering freshmen because the group had traded sexually explicit and other offensive messages in a Facebook group chat.[19] According to news reports, the members of the Facebook messaging group joked about rape, child abuse, and targeted others based on race, ethnicity, and nationality.[20] The attention that investigators must give to witnesses is difficult to overstate, but managing witnesses to ensure that helpful information is gathered from each witness is not a self-evident task. A student witness may be an alleged participant in misconduct or a person who otherwise is privy to the misconduct or observed the wrongdoing at issue. When interviewing a single witness the obvious goals include learning what actually happened, and preventing the recurrence of academic or behavioral misconduct. However, when potential witnesses include numerous students or the student misconduct investigation involves groups of students it is imperative that the investigators understand the special issues that come with large groups of potential witnesses. Be sure to:

- Contact all witnesses with potentially useful information. Create a log with identity, contact information, and brief written statements or questionnaires.

- Separate key witnesses from witnesses with information that is immaterial or is of limited significance to the investigation.
- Carefully consider the temptation to interview student witnesses together. Students listening to comments of others can be influenced to offer statements that are post-hoc rationalizations or simply offered to save face.
- Even if witnesses are interviewed separately, do not discount the possibility that witnesses may engage in collusion and privately attempt to align their statements prior to their independent interviews. This may be impossible to prevent but discouraging such collusion among witnesses may preserve the interview's integrity and demonstrate the investigator's effort to act in good faith.
- In the fog of an investigation with a large number of witnesses hold firm to assess the evidence, statements, or documents presented by each witness according to *relevance, credibility, and veracity.*

Document and Electronic Information Collection

The collection of documents relevant to the internal investigation should begin without delay. While a precise timeframe may involve speculation and not fit every situation, it should be understood that long delays detract from the institution's ability to respond to student misconduct. In some situations document collection and preservation may require the assistance of persons with specialized training in information technology and forensic analysis.[21] Having access to documents for review and study at the earliest stages of the investigation can provide a factual basis from which to identify witnesses to be interviewed, ensure that the investigation is proceeding consistent with its charge, and avoid learning disturbing facts during the closing phases of the investigation.

Thus, a document collection plan should be developed to guide the retrieval, custody, and analysis of hard-copy and electronic documents. Appropriate faculty, staff, other college or university employees, and investigators should work together to determine efficient methods to locate and collect relevant documents. Personnel familiar with computing technology and information systems may also be helpful in recovering documents available through institutional databases. However, involving such personnel in the investigation process should not result in disregard for chain of custody concerns and important priorities that include preserving electronic information and other data. (See also chapter 5.)

Consideration regarding what action may be taken to collect electronic or digital information should begin with an understanding of the institution's policies and practices regarding its network systems, digital communication infrastructure, and what is defined as appropriate computer usage for students at the college or university. Limited access, if any, may be available for electronic or digital information, images, videos, or audio representations generated by students outside the institution's resources that impacts internal investigations related to student misconduct.[22] Information generated through the internet, electronic devices, and other digital sources may be the most challenging for student affairs personal, university administrators, and executive leaders to capture because critical facts from video or audio depictions may be difficult to pinpoint in a timely manner.

Institutions such as Auburn University, the University of Oklahoma, and the University of Virginia have been the scene of recent alarming incidents involving allegations of student misconduct.[23] The University of Oklahoma incident is particularly noteworthy because the student misconduct centered on the video recording of a racist chant during a fraternity outing. The video later went viral after being posted on the internet and released to other outlets.[24] The collection of electronic information is certainly a complex area. When an investigation involves a substantive inquiry in this area it is necessary that the investigation team have access to personnel with the sophistication and skill to retrieve relevant data, documents, and other evidence.

Communicating with the Media

The 24-hour news cycle, the almost inherent unpredictability of student misconduct, the scope of student activities that occur on and off campus, among other concerns, places colleges and universities in a proverbial "fishbowl" to be scrutinized or judged without notice for their response to student misconduct crises. Given this reality triggered by the news commentators, social media, and the blogosphere, the internal investigation must be prepared to respond to media inquiries through the use of communications strategies that avoid derailing an investigation and, instead, project the institution's wherewithal to manage any potential instability. These strategies should be developed within the context of a crisis communication plan that ensures that the investigation team, university executives, student affairs personnel, and others who may find themselves the target of media questioning are equipped to respond to the media or understand what is necessary to get to an appropriate spokesperson for the institution. The ability to respond to the media, especially in a crisis, can demonstrate that the college or university and its leadership are competent and have the capacity to manage a particular controversy in a manner that communicates with the media, brings calm to the campus community that includes students, faculty, and alumni, and reassures concerned governmental officials and the general public. The failure to have a crisis communication plan in place can result in a public relations disaster for the university that can have tremendous consequences.

Best practices in crisis communication have been studied and tested by experts in various industries and professional fields with the predominant goal of mitigating the impact of the crisis on the institution.[25] A crisis communication plan may include guiding principles such as communicating with honesty and compassion, while remaining accessible to the media for updating and providing clarifications as needed.[26] As for responding to media inquiries related to a student misconduct investigation in particular, the following are helpful suggestions:

- Make every effort to anticipate and craft a response to potential questions before the student misconduct incident becomes newsworthy. Timing is important. Getting out in front of an issue can be invaluable.
- Be assertive and communicate solution-driven answers to media questions that have been vetted by the institution's student affairs leadership, which should include representation from the investigation team.
- An often-cited crisis management mantra—"tell it all, tell it early, and tell it yourself"—has some application in responding to media inquiries regarding student misconduct investigations. Telling the truth and taking on the tough questions matter.[27] Of course, this does not mean that legal obligations such as FERPA or other state and federal laws that impose disclosure limitations on an institution should be disregarded. The point here really emphasizes the importance of *responsible transparency*.
- Make sure that the main thing remains the main thing—caring for the general welfare of the students. In the thicket of regulatory compliance, avoiding legal liability, and dealing with the media, concern for the students can be overshadowed quickly. University spokespersons can prevent this from happening by assuring the student community that their well-being is

paramount. Using the response to media questions to speak directly to students and parents can pay huge dividends for the reputation of the college or university, and may even serve as a beacon that attracts future students.[28]

Investigations of student misconduct require attention to detail and an awareness of how to identify, collect, and verify information and facts important to the investigation. The approaches used to interview witnesses and collect documents and other pieces of evidence should be executed with deliberate forethought. Acting casually or based on one's own personal instincts is a clear path to missed opportunity and should be avoided.

Chapter 5

Confidentiality and Privilege

The Delta Phi Omega fraternity has been at the center of a hazing controversy at Western Louisiana University ("Western") for the last year. Several students who attempted to join the fraternity claimed that they were physically abused, forced to consume large amounts of alcohol, and hazed by student members of the fraternity during initiation activities. Five of the students quit the pledging process and have now sued the fraternity and Western for failing to protect them from personal injury and for refusing to investigate student misconduct by the Delta Phi Omega fraternity or other student organizations. These student plaintiffs claim that Western campus administrators knew of the potential for hazing but ignored the threat, and that the University has a long history of disregarding student misconduct.

The students filed a lawsuit in US District Court for the Middle District of Louisiana seeking monetary damages for violations of federal and state law. Consequently, lawyers representing the student plaintiffs submitted discovery requests demanding that Western disclose all records related to student misconduct, including internal investigation and counseling records pertaining to hazing charges raised against current and former Western students for the 2005–2016 academic years.

Lawyers for the students argue that the institution's investigation records are relevant to show that Western has demonstrated a pattern and practice of ignoring student misconduct, and that the University does not have, and historically has not established within its student code of conduct or elsewhere, rules and policies prohibiting hazing among student groups. In opposition to the students' discovery requests, Western contends that the disclosure of previous internal investigation reports or records involving student misconduct is prohibited by the attorney-client privilege because the internal investigations were conducted by University legal counsel in anticipation of litigation. Whether the internal investigation documents are subject to disclosure will be determined by the magistrate judge and will likely have serious implications for the scope of Western's legal liability.[1]

An internal investigation and related proceedings can be seen as a search for truth or easily criticized as a finger-pointing exercise. While there may be some legitimacy to each of these views, the internal investigation is more pragmatic in nature and when pursued in good faith its purpose is driven by the quest for tangible results. As a student misconduct internal investigation seeks to determine the validity of any alleged student wrongdoing, it also strives to impose proper remedial or corrective action without jeopardizing the institution's academic operations and community. But an investigative inquiry can lead to the discovery of sensitive information that a college or university may wish to protect from public disclosure. Therefore, colleges and universities working through legal counsel and student affairs administrators should be aware of the options that may be used to protect information, documents, or other tangible things produced during the course of an investigation.

Limiting access to confidential information is not necessarily an intuitive exercise but requires the cooperation of persons involved in the investigation process. Also, a keen sense of the institution's policies and practices is important, as well as relevant open records laws that require compliance despite any pragmatic interest in preventing disclosure of certain information or documents. For administrators acting within the scope of their professional duties, various protections may be available to defend their actions from a formal challenge. This chapter examines the legal concepts and doctrines used to limit the disclosure of certain communications and information and to insulate administrators and other key decision-makers from liability.

The Attorney-Client Privilege and Potential Waiver of the Privilege

At its core, a lawsuit is an adversarial dispute seeking resolution. The legal process provides a framework for these disputes to be heard and resolved by an impartial arbitrator or tribunal. In a civil dispute, as opposed to an action involving criminal charges, a properly filed complaint and responsive answer (the pleadings stage) is routinely followed by a period referred to as the discovery phase of the litigation. This occurs before the matter may be considered for trial.[2] During this pretrial phase of a lawsuit, the parties seek to identify evidence that is relevant to the complaint or defenses that may be raised but excludes evidence that is *privileged*. As a legal concept, privileges are used to protect confidential communications from disclosure or release. While the law does recognize privileges that protect communications between a husband and wife or a doctor and patient, the most well-known privilege may be the one between an attorney and a client.

The purpose of the attorney-client privilege is to encourage full and frank communication between attorneys and their clients and in so doing promote broader public interests in the observance of law and administration of justice. As a protective measure, confidential communications exchanged during an investigation that are not intended to be disclosed to third persons, other than persons involved in providing legal services, may be privileged. Communications between an attorney and his or her client have been determined to be the most deserving of protection. In *Upjohn Co. v. United States*, 449 U.S. 383, 389, 101 S. Ct. 677, 66 L. Ed.2d 584 (1981), long held as the leading US Supreme Court decision regarding the subject, the Court described the contours of the attorney-client privilege:

> the privilege applies only if (1) the asserted holder of the privilege is or sought to become a client; (2) the person to whom the communication was made (a) is a member of the bar of a court, or his subordinate and (b) in connection with this communication is acting as a lawyer; (3) the communication relates to a fact of which the attorney was informed (a) by his client (b) without the presence of strangers (c) for the purpose of securing primarily either (i) an opinion on law or (ii) legal services or (iii) assistance in some legal proceeding, and not (d) for the purpose of committing a crime or tort; and (4) the privilege has been (a) claimed and (b) not waived by the client.[3]

For the purpose of an internal investigation conducted at the direction of a college or university, the holder of the privilege will likely be the institution with the authority to determine whether communications remain privileged. While a college or university may choose to disclose sensitive information discovered as part of an internal investigation, failure to preserve the attorney-client privilege can have serious ramifications.

In August 2017, a lawyer representing women who alleged that they were raped at Baylor University successfully argued that the University waived the attorney-client privilege. A federal judge ordered Baylor University to release records, data, and an interview list from an investigation that found that the University mishandled allegations of sexual assault.[4] The University hired a private law firm to investigate the institution's handling of sexual assault cases after a student-athlete on the football team was accused of raping a student. Upon completion of the investigation, the University released a 13-page document listing the investigation's findings and recommendations. The University asserted that information provided to the outside law firm for purposes of the investigation was protected by the attorney-client privilege. However, the federal judge held that the University waived its protection under the attorney-client privilege when it publicly released the document summarizing details of the law firm's investigation.

Likewise, students who retain legal counsel to provide representation or legal advice during the course of a disciplinary proceeding may assert the attorney-client privilege. However, the formulaic nature of the *Upjohn* description of the attorney-client privilege should be viewed with care. It is important to note how easily the privilege can be waived by the presence of strangers to the communication or conduct that indicates that the communication was not considered confidential. Nonetheless, the privilege is not destroyed merely by the presence of others. Communications may remain protected when persons are present during a conversation between an attorney and his or her client if that person is needed to assist the attorney in providing legal services.[5]

Efforts to establish the attorney-client privilege in a student misconduct investigation should begin with the selection of legal counsel to conduct the investigation who will be acting as attorneys. More specifically, attorneys must be retained to provide legal advice in the context of the facts uncovered during the investigation. Confidential witness interviews and other inquiries should be conducted with the caveat that the attorney-investigators represent the college or university, and that the institution will make final decisions as to what communications are claimed as privileged. Reports and findings should not be disclosed to the public but rather should be shared with decision-makers in executive sessions. Initially, these terms should be set out in the attorney's engagement letter and should be emphasized at other points during the investigation as well as a necessary prerequisite.[6]

Work-Product Doctrine

As a general matter, the rules that govern the discovery phase of the litigation process are fairly liberal and are construed to permit the disclosure of relevant, non-privileged materials. The work-product doctrine functions as a restraint on the discovery rules similar to the attorney-client privilege but is distinguishable because the work-product doctrine is broader and technically not viewed as a privilege but as a qualified privilege.[7] The work-product doctrine protects documents, materials, information, and other work prepared by an attorney in anticipation of litigation from intrusion by an opposing attorney. The justification for the work-product doctrine emerged from the US Supreme Court decision in *Hickman v. Taylor*, 329 U.S. 495, 67 S. Ct. 385, 91 L. Ed. 451 (1947), where the court indicated that "the general policy against invading the privacy of an attorney's course of preparation is so well recognized and so essential to an orderly working of our system of legal procedure that a burden rests on the one who would invade that privacy to establish adequate reason to justify production through a subpoena or court order."[8]

The work-product doctrine does not provide blanket protection for information held by an attorney in all circumstances, including information generated for an internal investigation. The work-product doctrine will not apply where parties can show substantial necessity and undue hardship may result because materials sought are not otherwise available. However, a compelling question as to application of the work-product protection will center on whether the documents or materials were prepared in anticipation of litigation or in the ordinary course of institutional business. In *Long v. Anderson University*, 204 F.R.D. 129, 136 (S.D. Ind. 2001), a former student, Jeremy Long, and his mother sued the institution and several employees for alleged violation of Title IX of the Education Amendments of 1972 and made other federal and common law tort claims. As part of the discovery process, the plaintiffs requested documents related to an internal investigation conducted by the University regarding Long's harassment and discrimination complaint. Specifically, the plaintiffs' discovery request sought witness statements, notes, tape recordings, reports, and correspondence generated during the investigation, but the University objected to the discovery request and asserted protection under the work-product doctrine, arguing that the documents were prepared in anticipation of litigation. Addressing the application of the work-product doctrine relative to documents gathered as part of an internal investigation, the Indiana Federal District Court held that the plaintiffs were entitled to the documents relating to the internal investigation because the University had a harassment policy and the investigation was an ordinary and customary step in conducting its business, and the mere anticipation of litigation does not shield documents from production.[9]

Also, courts have considered whether materials generated as part of student disciplinary proceedings are protected by the work-protect doctrine. In *Dempsey v. Bucknell Univ.,* 296 F.R.D. 323, 330 (M.D. Pa. 2013), the court addressed whether a university's student conduct hearing constituted "litigation" to which work-product protection may have been applicable. The court held that the student conduct hearing process was adversarial in nature, involving a neutral tribunal empowered to adjudicate serious student misconduct charges. The process provided the opportunity to present evidence and witnesses, as well as opening and closing statements before a tribunal. The university proceedings were tantamount to litigation. Whether it was a governmental proceeding or an internal one provided by a private university was immaterial.

As for materials generated as part of a factual investigation, the work-product doctrine is applicable and disclosure may be allowed only where rare and exceptional circumstances can be shown. However, as indicated in the *Long* decision, courts may be unwilling to allow the work-product doctrine to interfere with the disclosure of documents prepared in the course of a university's ordinary business activities. To do so would invite institutions to exploit the work-product rule by allowing standard business practices, perhaps internal investigations, to appear to be action taken in anticipation of litigation.

An instructive clarification regarding what might constitute ordinary business activity that is not entitled to work-product protection versus action taken in anticipation of litigation and deserving of work-product protection can be found in *Soter v. Cowles Publ'g Co.,* 131 Wash. App. 882, 130 P.3d 840 (2006), aff'd, 162 Wash. 2d 716, 174 P.3d 60 (2007). In *Soter*, an elementary school student died from an allergic reaction after being given a peanut-based snack during a field trip. The incident triggered a school district investigation and an eventual wrongful death lawsuit that resulted in a settlement. In the aftermath, a local newspaper sought records of the school district's investigation of the incident under the state's public disclosure act, but the school district claimed that the investigation materials were exempt from disclosure as attorney work-product. The court agreed with the school district's finding that "specific litigation was anticipated from the outset."[10] Among the facts the court found compelling was that immediately following the student's death the school district contacted a lawyer and retained an investigator in anticipation of a wrongful death action. Moreover, the court recognized that documents created by the school district prior to the student's death and given to their lawyers in anticipation of litigation were not work-product. The court made clear that pre-existing records would not be granted work-product protection but stated that "[w]e are reviewing records prepared by counsel, after the fact, solely for the defense of anticipated litigation."[11]

On appeal, the Supreme Court of Washington noted that on multiple occasions the US Supreme Court has indicated that "'[f]orcing an attorney to disclose notes and memoranda of witnesses' oral statements is particularly disfavored because it tends to reveal the attorney's mental processes.' *Upjohn,* 449 U.S. at 399, 101 S. Ct. 677; *Hickman,* 329 U.S. at 513, 67 S. Ct. 385."[12] With respect to the obligations of a state agency, in this case a public educational institution, to share investigation materials in anticipation of litigation, the court observed the following:

> *The Spokesman-Review* and amici assert that if we affirm the Court of Appeals based either on work product or attorney client privilege, agencies will be encouraged to hand contentious or potentially embarrassing investigations over to their attorneys to avoid public disclosure. As the Court of Appeals noted, the school district fully acknowledges the need for liberal access to agency information, but ***the school district also raises its countervailing duty to safeguard the public treasury by aggressively defending itself against civil liability.*** Soter, 131 Wash. App. at 905, 130 P.3d 840. It is essential that lawyers representing our public agencies work with a certain degree of privacy free from unnecessary intrusion, in order to assemble information, sift what they consider to be the relevant from the irrelevant facts, prepare legal theories, and plan strategy without undue interference. *See Hickman,* 329 U.S. at 510-11, 67 S. Ct. 385. Soter v. Cowles Pub. Co., Wash. 2d 716, 748-49 (Wash., 2007), 174 P.3d 60, 77, 162 (emphasis added).

In the case of colleges and universities confronted with the realities of civil liability that can flow from student misconduct, the need for investigative proceedings to consider the protection provided by the work-product doctrine shall remain an important investigative and student affairs consideration for the foreseeable future.

The Self-Critical Evaluation Privilege

The self-critical evaluation privilege[13] seeks to limit the disclosure and grant protection to investigations and reviews that critique internal policy, processes, and other organizational operations.

> [I]n its broadest terms, the "privilege" has been stated to apply "to any critique by a person or entity of its own operations, policies or processes." *Cloud v. Superior Court of Los Angeles*, 50 Cal. App. 4 1552 (1996). Stated another way, this "privilege" concerns situations where "if a party has conducted a confidential analysis of its own performance in a matter implicating a substantial public interest, with a view towards correction of errors, the disclosure of that analysis in the context of litigation may deter the party from conducting such a candid review in the future." *Robinson* v. *United States*, 205 F.R.D. 104 (W.D. N.Y. 2001).[14]

While garnering less attention than the attorney-client privilege or the work-product doctrine, the self-critical evaluation privilege deserves consideration for at least two reasons that impact the higher education community. First, it is apparent that colleges and universities are and probably will remain under increasing regulatory pressure for the foreseeable future. For example, the US Department of Education remains steadfast in its position to hold accrediting agencies accountable regarding various performance metrics which will trigger colleges and universities to conduct more internal audits and investigations to assess the institution's performance or compliance in multiple areas.[15] To the extent an institution wishes to keep such information confidential, the self-critical evaluation privilege may be a valuable tool. Second, Enterprise Risk Management (ERM) has taken center stage at colleges and universities across the country as the strategy of choice to minimize institutional risk. Enterprise risk management urges campus leaders to merge efforts regarding institutional governance, management operations, and the institution's strategic objectives by applying lessons learned from other disciplines and industries to mitigate liability or potential risks.[16] Going forward, internal investigations, programmatic reviews, self-study exercises, and similar activities are likely to be utilized with increasing frequency to advance enterprise risk management goals. Here again, the self-critical evaluation privilege may be an attractive method to limit access to internal evaluations prepared for ERM purposes.

Although state and federal courts have acknowledged the self-critical evaluation privilege, institutions may waive the privilege where documents or information seeking protection were not prepared with an expectation that they would be kept in a confidential manner.[17] In *University of Kentucky v. Courier-Journal & Louisville Times Co.*, 830 S.W.2d 373, 374-75 (Ky. 1992), news media outlets, including the *Louisville Courier-Journal*, brought a declaratory action to determine whether a report prepared by the University of Kentucky in response to alleged NCAA rules violations were subject to disclosure under the Kentucky Open Records Act, KRS 61.870, *et seq.* Among the defenses raised, the University argued that the "doctrine of self-critical analysis makes the Response privileged at common law and exempt from the disclosure requirements of the Act."[18] The court disagreed. While finding that the Open Records Act preempted common law and that the self-critical analysis did not apply in matters regarding disclosure of public records, the court held that the University waived the self-critical analysis privilege by disclosing the report to the NCAA—a private voluntary unincorporated association. The self-critical evaluation privilege is intended to advance the free flow of information but courts may be reluctant to protect internal investigation materials that were not prepared with the expectation that information produced as part of an internal investigation would be kept confidential. Therefore, the attorney-client privilege, work-product doctrine, and the self-critical evaluation privilege may offer some protection for documents, data, statements, or reports produced during the course of an investigation, but these protections must be executed with particularity and can be easily waived for legitimate reasons such as regulatory compliance or transparency. This is an important matter to ponder prior to and throughout a misconduct investigation involving students.

Freedom of Information Act (FOIA) and Open Records Law

The federal Freedom of Information Act (FOIA), 5 U.S.C §552 (2006), and open records laws enacted by states across the country share the same general purpose—to open governmental records to public scrutiny. These laws are intended to grant citizens full and complete information regarding government affairs as well as the official actions taken by public officials and public employees. Public agencies, including public colleges and universities, are required to make documents available to the public upon request, unless an exception is applicable. FOIA is construed liberally to open governmental records to allow public scrutiny, while exceptions to the law are viewed narrowly. However, FOIA is not intended to cause an unwarranted invasion of personal privacy. To a notable degree, state open record laws are patterned after FOIA, and when a unique open records issue arises at the state level courts frequently turn to the federal law for guidance, *Harwood v. McDonough,* 344 Ill. App.3d 242, 248, 279 Ill. Dec. 56, 799 N.E.2d 859, 864 (2003).

Procedurally, FOIA places the burden on a public entity seeking to deny access to the government files to show that the requested documents are exempt from disclosure under the statute.[19] Moreover, the public agency must provide clear and convincing evidence and sufficient details supporting application of the exemption. Judges are also free to conduct an *in camera* inspection of the files or documents at issue to determine whether the governmental entity satisfies its burden of proof.[20] In *State Journal-Register v. University of Illinois Springfield,* 994 N.E.2d

705, 712-13 (Ill. App. 4th Dist.,2013), an Illinois court considered whether documents related to the resignations of university coaches who were allegedly involved in a sexual assault incident during a women's softball team trip in 2009 were exempt from disclosure under the Illinois FOIA. The incident garnered media attention, which led the *State Journal-Register* ("Journal") to submit two FOIA requests for documents related to the coaches' resignations. The University of Illinois-Springfield declined to comply with the FOIA requests, which led to a lawsuit filed by the Journal wherein the court held that certain internal communications and witness statements were not subject to exemption but many of the documents were protected from disclosure.[21]

Many exceptions or exemptions to FOIA or state open records laws are designed to serve confidentiality or privacy concerns that are determined to be in the public interest. Typical exceptions prevent disclosure of medical information, employee personnel files, and police investigative materials, which lawmakers believe frequently include sensitive information that need not be disclosed to the general public. There is some debate as to whether FOIA requests or open records requests for student records are barred from disclosure under FERPA.[22] Some courts have held that FERPA is not a law that prohibits the disclosure of educational records but a provision that imposes a penalty for the disclosure of educational records.[23] In *Red & Black Publishing Co. v. Board of Regents*, 427 S.E.2d 257, 261 (Ga. 1993), the University of Georgia student newspaper sought access to documents and records of the institution's student Organization Court specifically related to hazing charges against a social fraternity. The Supreme Court of Georgia held that the student newspaper was entitled to the records requested and that FERPA did not apply because the requested information did not constitute educational records such as academic performance records, financial aid documents, or other sensitive student information. According to the Georgia court, the documents involved were not the type that FERPA was intended to protect and were subject to the Georgia Opens Records Act.[24]

But other courts have found that FERPA provides a sound basis for denying access to student information.[25] In *U.S. v. Miami*, 294 F.3d 797, 804 (6th Cir. 2002), the US Department of Justice acting on behalf of the Department of Education (DOE) filed an action against Miami University and the Ohio State University seeking to prevent the Universities from releasing disciplinary records that included personally identifiable student information in violation of FERPA. Agreeing with the DOE, the federal district court for the Southern District of Ohio granted an injunction permanently enjoining the universities from releasing student disciplinary records in violation of FERPA. On appeal, the Sixth Circuit affirmed the lower court, confirming that student disciplinary records were protected by FERPA.

> Under a plain language interpretation of the FERPA, student disciplinary records are education records because they directly relate to a student and are kept by that student's university. . . . In fact, a detailed study of the statute and its evolution by amendment reveals that Congress intends to include student disciplinary records within the meaning of "education records" as defined by the FERPA. This intention is evinced by a review of the express statutory exemptions from privacy and exceptions to the definition of "education records." *United States v. Miami Univ.*, 294 F.3d 797, 812 (6th Cir. 2002).

FOIA requests can pose a serious challenge for public colleges or universities charged with investigating student misconduct disputes that may examine or uncover sensitive information regarding a student's educational record. For many institutions, whether FERPA represents an effective defense against open records requests will turn on a detailed reading of the state's open records law or FOIA statute. In matters where only the federal FOIA law is at issue, it remains an unsettled question whether FERPA acts as an absolute bar to FOIA requests.[26]

However, in *Press-Citizen Company Inc. v. University of Iowa*, 817 N.W.2d 480 (Iowa 2012), the Supreme Court of Iowa framed the legal question around the fundamental meaning of FERPA as a federal law. In this case, the Press-Citizen Company (a newspaper publisher) sought the disclosure of records regarding a sexual assault investigation involving student-athletes. The University did release some documents but determined that certain categories of documents would not be released because they were confidential and protected by FERPA.[27] Arguments raised by the parties specifically required the court to examine the interplay between FERPA and the state's open records law. The Press-Citizen argued that FERPA does not prohibit disclosure of educational records but only operates to withhold federal funding from educational institutions that have policies and practices that permit the release of education records without consent or other conditions set out under FERPA.[28] The University contended that FERPA represented positive law—statutory manmade law—not merely a funding provision triggered by institutional action. When compared with the authority set out by the Iowa Open Records Act, the University also argued that FERPA required confidentiality as a matter of federal supremacy.[29] While recognizing that many jurisdictions across the country were divided on the import of FERPA, the Supreme Court of Iowa resolved that in this case the state law itself incorporated a confidentiality obligation that recognized FERPA and thereby nullified previous orders requiring the University to produce certain categories of documents.

Student misconduct investigations can draw the attention of activists, media outlets, and other groups interested in gaining access to documents and information through a FOIA request. For public institutions of higher education, the internal investigation process should include a thorough examination of FOIA exemptions or open records act exceptions that may be available to avoid releasing sensitive information that is the subject of a student misconduct investigation. Many of these exceptions were amendments to existing law approved by various state legislatures and Congress in the belief that the public interest was better served by confidentiality in some cases, and that privacy interests of individuals subject to some form of government records should be protected.[30]

Likewise, for public colleges and universities it is necessary and prudent that internal investigations and the materials generated as a result of an investigation be considered as materials subject to open records laws. Because open records laws can grant numerous groups access to internal investigation documents, it should be expected that open records requests will be vigorously pursued. Understanding the mechanics that apply to requests for campus investigation materials, and the exceptions that might prohibit public disclosure, is critical and can perhaps serve as an important shield for the campus officials, students, and, in some circumstances, the public.

Preserving Documents and the Litigation Hold

An internal investigation can be the catalyst for a variety of events intended to minimize harm to the educational community. But at the same time, it can trigger obligations to retain and preserve certain information to limit the institution's exposure to legal liability. The duty to preserve documents or other information relevant to student misconduct allegations is among the obligations that investigators and university counsel should give careful consideration.[31] Courts have found that the duty to preserve documents arises "when a party should have known that the evidence may be relevant to future litigation." *Zubulake v. UBS Warburg LLC,* 220 F.R.D. 212, 216 (S.D.N.Y. 2003). While incidents of student misconduct may not always result in litigation, the potential for litigation to ensue does exist especially where the consequences for a student's career or long-term future are at stake.

Moreover, the failure to preserve materials, information, or data that may be used as evidence in foreseeable litigation as well as the destruction of evidence can result in sanctions and spoliation claims.[32] In *Doe v. Norwalk Community College,* 248 F.R.D. 372, 231 Ed. Law Rep. 292 (D. Conn. 2007), a student who was allegedly sexually harassed and assaulted by a professor filed a lawsuit against the college and the professor, alleging violations of Title IX regarding the sexual misconduct and other state law tort claims. Also, the student sought sanctions against the College for discovery misconduct and spoliation of evidence. Addressing the College's failure to preserve relevant evidence, the Court observed that the duty to preserve evidence related to the sexual assault allegation arose when academic administrators and faculty initially met to discuss the allegations prior to the student's action of filing the lawsuit. Hence, "'[t]he duty to preserve attached at the time that litigation was reasonably anticipated.' *Zubulake,* 220 F.R.D. at 217. At that time, the defendants 'must suspend [their] routine document retention/destruction policy and put in place a "litigation hold" to ensure the preservation of relevant documents.' *Zubulake,* 220 F.R.D. at 218."[33]

The duty to preserve documents and related information, therefore, represents a continuing obligation for internal investigations where the likelihood of litigation is foreseeable. Generally a litigation-hold action is a directive for employees, staff, or related personnel to retain and not destroy documents or electronic communications that may be of importance in an anticipated or pending dispute. This attempt to preserve documents and electronic communications typically functions as a notice that informs persons with the power to control the continued existence of electronic information and documents of the need to retain the information.[34]

The execution of a litigation hold at a college or university can be a daunting task for various reasons. First, institutions of higher education generally are decentralized organizations with information and documents generated or produced from multiple sources. Next, the personnel or custodians of information critical to an internal investigation or any potential litigation often have independent and overlapping functions that coexist within a management structure that may be bureaucratic in nature or use less formal administrative methods. For example, the Office of Public Safety may have the capacity to produce and preserve documents and information about a student misconduct incident more efficiently than the Student Activities Office or Office of Multicultural Affairs. It is also important to recognize that persons with custody or access to student investigation materials should have the necessary guidance to preserve important documents.[35] Typical challenges may involve executing a litigation hold wherein the information sought is not held by an administrative unit but by a faculty member who operates independently and with a substantial degree of freedom. Regardless of the custodial source, the campus officials should have well-defined document preservation procedures.

A Final Word about Privileges and Managing Confidential Communication

While the purpose of an investigation is to seek out and collect information regarding misconduct allegations, investigators, student affairs administrators, and attorneys acting on behalf of the institution should be cognizant of opportunities to preserve privileges that can limit access and disclosure of certain information. Of course, an institution may choose to waive or simply not exercise an option to protect information. But that decision should be made knowingly with a reasonable understanding of the potential consequences and not inadvertently or because parties conducting the investigation failed to confer with campus officials regarding the institution's legal right to limit disclosure of confidential information.

Campus administrators should also understand that participating in an internal investigation can lead various stakeholders to carefully scrutinize the action of individual administrators or personnel retained to conduct an internal investigation. Investigators can be charged with unlawful conduct and find themselves personally liable for actions taken in the course of an internal investigation. In 2017, a Baylor University athletics employee sued investigators for negligence regarding the institution's review of a sexual assault incident. Accord to the lawsuit, Baylor conducted a sub-par investigation that led to an incomplete and libelous report, which resulted in the employee's termination.[36] In a similar action at Penn State University, the institution's president was dismissed in the aftermath of a tremendous scandal that got national attention regarding criminal misconduct by a former football coach that involved inappropriate contact with minors. While Penn State conducted an investigation to determine the veracity of the alleged misconduct and the involvement of university officials, the former president responded by filing a lawsuit in state court against Penn State for defamation, claiming that the investigation included misrepresentations regarding his actions.[37] For college and university administrators at public institutions, qualified immunity may be available to shield administrators from civil liability and civil damages. Pursuant to the qualified immunity doctrine, state or government officials performing discretionary functions can avoid liability unless there is evidence that their conduct violates clearly established statutory or constitutional rights.[38] Put another way, officials at state-supported college and universities performing discretionary functions in their official capacity can rely on qualified immunity from civil suits for damages unless they act with knowledge, or some reasonable awareness, that their conduct violated a person's clearly established constitutional rights.[39]

In *De Jong v. Metro. State Univ.*, No. A12-0829, 2012 WL 5990306, at *4 (Minn. Ct. App. Dec. 3, 2012), at issue were statements made during an internal investigation conducted by a vice president for student affairs at Metropolitan State University (MSU) in Minnesota. This investigation followed an angry exchange between De Jong, a student at MSU, and her instructors in the alcohol and drug counselor program at the University. MSU's internal investigation of the incident resulted in a written report that indicated that De Jong violated the student conduct code and triggered numerous sanctions, including conduct probation.[40] The student responded by filing a defamation suit in state court that was dismissed based on summary judgment. Among the reasons relied upon by the court was the absence of any evidence that allegedly defamatory statements as to the student's reputation were published externally. Statements regarding the investigation were only shared with persons responsible for the investigation and subsequent disciplinary proceeding and, therefore, protected as a qualified privilege. Internal communications (intra-company or intra-corporate communications) based on a proper or reasonable motive made during an internal investigation are generally privileged unless actual malice can be shown. In this case, the court found that the statements secured during the investigation were logical and necessary inquiries, and that the University proceeded in a reasonably prudent fashion. Although the investigation did include some negative commentary as to the student involved, there was no evidence of actual malice that showed direct proof of personal spite. Thus, any allegedly defamatory statements internally published during the investigation were protected by qualified privilege.

Careful decision-making regarding the collection and disclosure of statements pertinent to the student misconduct internal investigation cannot be taken for granted. Administrators and internal investigators should understand custodial responsibilities related to confidential communications (and applicable legal doctrines such as qualified immunity) and that qualified privilege can provide insulation from personal liability—which has value even if only in the interest of self-preservation. However, these protections can also be waived, sometimes inadvertently or even in a noble effort to demonstrate institutional transparency. Therefore, caution and a working familiarity with these legal concepts is vital for those higher education professionals engaged in the internal investigation process.

Chapter 6

Results and Outcomes

Paul Bronson, a student at Northern University (NU) was in good academic standing and scheduled to graduate at the end of the semester with a bachelor's degree in communications. His longtime girlfriend, Amy Carter, was also scheduled to graduate in the spring, but with honors and a dual degree in finance and mathematics. Unfortunately, the relationship between Paul and Amy came to an abrupt end a few weeks ago when Amy discovered that Paul was romantically involved with another female undergraduate student.

In their final semester Paul and Amy had decided to take a class together in political science (P.S. 300) that required an extensive research paper. Both Paul and Amy chose to write about the rise of voter suppression laws in national elections. Their instructor, Professor David Smith, reviewed all student papers submitted in the course and found the papers by Paul and Amy to be extraordinarily similar. Professor Smith reported his concerns as a likely plagiarism violation to the chairperson for the Political Science Department and the Dean's Office. Professor Smith and the Department Chair, Dr. Ed Tolbert, hastily investigated the matter and, relying heavily on Amy's strong academic record, determined that Paul Bronson had plagiarized the paper prepared by Amy Carter for the P.S. 300 course.

Paul was charged with academic dishonesty and misconduct and a disciplinary hearing was held, which resulted in his expulsion. Paul appealed the expulsion decision to the Provost at NU, who has the authority to review all evidence—whether collected during the investigation or presented during the hearing—and may reverse academic disciplinary decisions that are not supported by the evidence. In the course of considering Paul's appeal, the Provost reviewed the content of the research papers prepared by the two students involved, as well as the electronic versions of the documents that were stored on Paul Bronson's computer and Amy Carter's computer. The electronic files produced as a result of the investigation included date-stamped files that indicated when the documents were created and saved. The Provost's review of the computer files revealed that Paul Bronson's paper was created and saved on dates *before* Amy Carter created and saved her paper on her personal computer.

Thus, based on the review conducted pursuant to Paul Bronson's appeal, the Provost was compelled to reverse the decision expelling Paul from Northern University because the disciplinary action was not supported by adequate evidence.[1]

Student misconduct investigations have consequences. The results, outcomes, findings, or observations cited in a written investigation report can completely derail a student's future, lead to an employee's termination, or harm an institution's reputation. But the results of an internal investigation can also exonerate an alleged perpetrator or aid a university in implementing preventive measures that are in the best interest of all students. And because higher education has to be about more than earning credentials and disciplining students, colleges and universities should be urged to use the results of an internal investigation to encourage students. This chapter considers the student's right to counsel, articulation of the student misconduct charge, and other concerns that influence the outcome of a student misconduct investigation.

Application of Due Process Standard with the Accused and Advocates

When an institution reaches a decision to take disciplinary action against a student for misconduct it should be anticipated that the decision will be scrutinized or called into question. The best defensive response often relies on the institution's ability to demonstrate that (1) a thorough investigation process was undertaken by the college or university consistent with the institution's internal policies and best practices, and (2) that the student or students accused of misconduct were at least afforded minimal procedural due process. From a legalistic viewpoint, this refers to providing the accused with notice of the charges, giving the student an opportunity to respond, allowing him or her to have an advisor present in a disciplinary hearing, and offering the student the right to appeal. However, there are other important objectives that an investigation can achieve, such as pointing out a pathway for correcting behavior and giving student affairs personnel valuable information to prevent a recurrence of student misconduct. Also, due process is an important standard that ought to remind all persons involved in the disciplinary process that fairness and impartiality will guide the investigation and other proceedings.

Institutional Mission and Student Discipline

The mission of an institution of higher education is to offer programs and activities that allow students to develop socially and intellectually so that they are equipped to pursue their professional and personal life goals without reservations. For some students, however, college is nothing more than a self-imposed diversion that concentrates not on scholastic achievement but is focused on socializing. In the popular movie *Forrest Gump*, one of the central characters is a female undergraduate student named Jenny who finds herself searching for romance and dreaming of becoming a folk singer. As depicted in the movie,

Jenny's college years were quickly brushed aside in exchange for cross-country road trips, experimentation with illegal drugs, sexual encounters, and partying. Put another way, the traditional college experience available to Jenny did not compete well with other opportunities and temptations of interest to her.

For students like Jenny who make choices that lead to behavior that falls outside the parameters of permissible conduct as defined by an academic institution, student disciplinary proceedings provide a system for adjudicating student conduct. The intent is not to punish or restrict a person's liberty interest but to correct a student's conduct so that he or she can again focus on academic goals and achieve the finer things that life can offer.[2]

Right to Counsel

Student misconduct proceedings can result in a range of consequences. Minor infractions can bring about warnings or voluntary agreements that require student consultations with counselors or student affairs staff to correct behavior and minimize recurring misconduct. More serious misconduct can reach beyond violations of campus regulations to include criminal acts that may result in fines or even incarceration. Where college or university disciplinary proceedings are triggered, including investigations, consequences are influenced by what a student says, how a student answers questions, or what written statements the student submits to investigators and campus administrators. At least two conclusions are possible: a student can be vindicated and found innocent of any alleged misconduct or a student can be found to have breached rules or policies that may justify a student's suspension, expulsion, or other sanctions from the college or university.

Some commentators have acknowledged that where criminal prosecution may flow from student misconduct, the need for a student to have the aid of an attorney may be greater because of the complexity of legal issues raised by a pending criminal case.[3] In light of this possibility, it is important to note that granting a student the right to legal counsel can have limitations. For instance, allowing a student the right to legal counsel as an advisor does not permit a student the unfettered right to have his or her lawyer fully participate in campus investigatory or disciplinary proceedings.

Courts examining due process concerns for students involved in disciplinary proceedings have not declared that students have an absolute right to counsel.[4] At best, courts have been divided regarding a student's right to have legal representation during a disciplinary proceeding. In *French v. Bashful*, 303 F. Supp. 1333, 1337 (E.D. La. 1969), students who in May of 1969 participated in an on-campus protest, sit-in, and alleged takeover of administrative offices at Southern University at New Orleans (SUNO), a public university, challenged expulsion and suspension penalties imposed by the institution's disciplinary committee. The students alleged, inter alia, that they were denied due process because the university refused to allow the students' legal counsel to represent them at disciplinary hearings held on May 9 and June 2 of 1969. Relying on the Fifth Circuit's decision in *Dixon v. Alabama State Board of Education*, 294 F.2d 150, 158–159 (5th Cir. 1961), wherein the court expressed guidelines for student disciplinary proceedings, the district court recognized that the jurisprudence as to the student's right to counsel was thin and while there was some support for granting students the right to legal counsel it was not identified in *Dixon* as a necessary element of procedural due process.[5] Furthermore, the court in *French* believed that the SUNO students received a fair hearing, consistent with the protections set out in *Dixon*, but ultimately held that the students were denied due process when they were not allowed to have their attorneys assist them at the hearing. In this case, the students were not reinstated but were granted a new hearing in which their legal counsel was allowed to participate.

Some commentators have agreed that beyond the constitutional protections that support the assistance of counsel in criminal proceedings authorized by the Sixth Amendment to the

US Constitution, students should be afforded the right to counsel where the institution is acting through a lawyer, as well as in trial-type proceedings, and perhaps where there is a material threat to a student's pursuit of a college education as a consequence of a suspension or expulsion penalties.[6] However, whether a student has a right to have legal counsel present during an interview conducted as part of a fact-finding student misconduct investigation is not absolute. Colleges and universities may differ for various reasons on this issue. Certainly the pre-hearing phase of a student disciplinary proceeding should be executed with caution. Opportunities to de-escalate tensions and impose practical solutions should be carefully considered and taken advantage of when feasible for the students involved and the institution. In this regard, some legal scholars have contended that allowing a student the right to counsel may have practical benefits:

> Two other factors, apart from a lawyer's special talents, strengthen our conviction that lawyers cannot in fairness be shut out of the process. First, forbidding a student counsel may well erect a one-way barrier; the rules do not prevent the school from turning for advice to its own Office of Legal Counsel, and we know that such contact often occurs. Counsel may not formally appear; yet she is only a telephone call away. Because there is no practical method to forestall these off-the-record contacts, we see no reason, a fortiori, why students should not be allowed them. Second, regardless of any constraint, some students will still consult a family attorney or lawyer acquaintance; in the circumstances, this is hardly surprising. Moreover, once consulted, the lawyer may remain in the near background, hidden but present. Given that reality—and once again there is no practical way to forestall it—why shouldn't the lawyer be allowed to emerge into the open, to advise her client without the client's fearing that in defending himself against a violation of the rules, he may be infringing the rule against counsel?[7]

Students facing disciplinary charges can feel overwhelmed when confronted with the force and authority of the institution to such a degree that the presence of an attorney seated in the interview room can have a calming or leveling effect that lends aid to the student. Moreover, allowing a student to have a retained attorney present during an investigatory interview can assist the student in offering thoughtful responses or opting to remain silent.[8] The challenges that can surface, however, involve conflict that might also be caused by the attorney's presence during the interview, especially where the interests of the student and her legal counsel seek to unduly influence the fact-finding effort. For this reason, investigators should consult with university legal counsel in situations where a student seeks to invite an attorney into an interview or investigation setting.

Restorative Justice

Student conduct investigations perform an important fact-finding function but it would be a serious mistake and a missed opportunity to frame the student misconduct investigation as a data-gathering process designed to simply impose penalties or disciplinary action.[9] Rather, the results of a student misconduct investigation should be viewed as an opportunity for change, to improve the condition of a campus environment, and to help students grow in a manner that equates to maturity—not just to point out wrongdoing but to guide students to a better path. The restorative justice movement has given voice to a view that student disciplinary matters should be more than a punishment determination process. Restorative justice is not fixated on punishment but rather on mitigating the harm, holding the perpetrators accountable, and healing the community. This calls for an intentional effort to balance complying with campus policies and legal mandates with searching for opportunities to facilitate healing among the persons involved and the campus community.

The relationship between a college or university and its students should be a lifetime affiliation that evolves through various levels and labels. While the relationship with the school begins with degree-achievement classifications such as undergraduate or graduate student, it is anticipated that students will go on to become active alumni and perhaps even take on the role of donor by virtue of some contribution to the institution. We hope the very best for all students who enroll in our institutions of higher education, and the best for their relationship with the institution. When students confront misconduct allegations during the course of their matriculation, the reality of rule breaking should not be taken lightly and students may be subject to suspension, dismissal, or other sanctions. Put another way, the consequences of student misconduct jeopardize a student's potential lifelong relationship with the institution and all the benefits that may be available from the student-university relationship.

Therefore, the restorative justice approach would entail that a student misconduct investigation should not simply be seen as a preliminary step in an exclusively adversarial process designed to dole out punishment. While some might argue that our criminal justice system is well served by the adversarial nature of judicial proceedings in our courts, the prosecution of criminal matters differs from what our objectives should be regarding efforts to resolve student conduct problems. The following offers practical examples of steps student affairs professionals and academic administrators can take to integrate restorative justice principles into the student misconduct investigation processes.

De-emphasize punitive and disciplinary action and promote accountability and personal responsibility. The campus student misconduct investigation and disciplinary proceedings cannot be perceived as a retaliatory system. Instead, students should be urged to come forward with honest information relevant to a misconduct investigation. This is the ultimate win-win.

Students become part of the solution and administrators gain important allies in the quest to advance positive student conduct.

Facilitate dialogue that leads to better decisions. Student leaders, faculty, and administrators should be offered an opportunity to share their perspectives on student misconduct (e.g., academic integrity, substance abuse, sexual assault, or micro-aggressions) and the importance of collective action by members of the campus community.

Learn from student misconduct, especially the most egregious. Where a student is found to have breached campus policies or regulations, opportunities to restore the student should not be abandoned. Any punishment or penalty imposed on a student should consider a pathway that allows the student to return to campus and complete his or her academic program. If such a recommendation is not available, there should be some assessment of the threat posed to the institution and why the threat was not detected prior to the student misconduct incident. To the extent possible, the internal investigation should seek to pinpoint not just what campus rules were violated but the factors that contributed to the problematic student behavior.

Implementing restorative justice ideals adds value to the results of an internal investigation. Student misconduct and problematic behavior are realities but should not be a catalyst for punitive action. For most students, a misconduct incident ought to be viewed as a distraction from the ultimate goal—the completion of a student's college education. When an investigation uncovers student misconduct, the next question is whether the action that functions as a distraction is so severe that the student is no longer fit to matriculate toward degree completion. Assuming the answer is no, the college or university should be compelled to find a way forward for the student and all those involved.

Articulating and Establishing the Student Misconduct Charge

As discussed in chapter 1, due process requires that students charged for misconduct and subject to disciplinary action be given notice of an alleged violation and a chance to respond. An institution's decision to pursue misconduct charges that may result in student sanctions or penalties creates a basic obligation that the misconduct charges be articulated with clarity so that the accused student can respond to the allegations. It is here that the internal investigation can perform an important function: pairing the *specific misconduct* with campus rules and regulations that may determine a student's guilt as opposed to proffering *generalized or conclusory allegations* that can lead to unjustified student misconduct charges. The inability to link prohibited behavior, as defined by a student handbook or code of conduct, to specific factual findings can undermine or even discredit student disciplinary proceedings. In *Boyd v. State Univ. of New York at Cortland*, 110 A.D.3d 1174, 973 N.Y.S.2d 413, (2013), a student enrolled at State University of New York (SUNY) at Cortland was charged with harassing a female student attending the University of Delaware. The factual allegations supporting the charge indicated that the harassment was defined as threatening phone calls, text messages, and other behavior directed at the female student. Following a disciplinary hearing, a recommendation was made to permanently dismiss the accused student for violating SUNY's Code of Student Conduct and demonstrating a failure to comply with federal, state, and local laws. The recommendation was appealed to the Vice President for Student Services but the findings were upheld and, thereafter, the student filed an action in state court seeking to annul the disciplinary determination.

Among the arguments raised by the student charged with unlawful harassment was the contention that he was denied due process because the University's disciplinary action was not supported by detailed factual findings. Agreeing with the student's contention, the court found that the University's claims of harassment and threats directed toward the female student were only supported by conclusory statements and failed to set forth specific conduct that constituted a basis for determining guilt with respect to the code of student conduct or findings that a crime was committed under Delaware law.[10] As for what the law does require, the importance of the fact-finding function for student misconduct investigations is enormous.

> In a disciplinary proceeding at a public institution of higher education, due process entitles a student accused of misconduct to "a statement detailing the factual findings and the evidence relied upon by the decision-maker in reaching the determination of guilt" (*Matter of Kalinsky v. State Univ. of N.Y. at Binghamton,* 161 A.D.2d 1006, 1007, 557 N.Y.S.2d 577 [1990]; *see Matter of Schwarzmueller v. State Univ. of N.Y. at Potsdam,* 105 A.D.3d 1117, 1119, 962 N.Y.S.2d 752; *Matter of Rauer v. State Univ. of N.Y., Univ. at Albany,* 159 A.D.2d 835, 836, 552 N.Y.S.2d 983 [1990]).[11]

This does not suggest that documents articulating standards of student conduct need to become binding, enforceable agreements. Student codes of conduct have been understood as a pledge that students are expected to acknowledge and adhere to during their matriculation. Consequently, such codes serve as a benchmark for expected student conduct that can guide results of an internal investigation and ensure that factual findings are based on legitimate objective standards. See *Shinabargar v. Bd. of Trustees of Univ. of D.C.,* 164 F. Supp. 3d 1, 29 (D.D.C. 2016), which indicated that a university's honor system was merely an acknowledgment or pledge that a student would become familiar with the student handbook and seek to abide by the academic norms and standards expressed by the honor system. In short, the UDC Honor Code was not an enforceable contract.

Advancing Investigation Integrity through Cooperation with Campus Safety Departments

On- and off-campus student misconduct disputes can and often do involve the work of campus police officers. The role of the campus law enforcement officer has evolved over time, seemingly in rhythm with the growth and development of postsecondary institutions. The primary work of campus police or campus safety departments began with basic activities that centered on watchman duties that included protecting campus facilities from fire, flood, or other forms of mayhem.[12] Prior to World War II, the simplicity of the watchman system offered a reasonable approach to campus safety that would come under increasing pressure as student enrollment soared in the 1950s and an unprecedented period of student unrest and campus demonstrations erupted in the 1960s and 1970s.[13] As a result, the activities of the campus police department have grown in scope and complexity to include emergency preparedness training, active shooter response capabilities, coordination with campus threat assessment teams, and other functions.[14]

During this timeframe, organizations such as the International Association of Campus Law Enforcement Administrators (IACLEA) have emerged with a focus on addressing the challenges confronting campus law enforcement. Among IACLEA's noteworthy contributions are the best practices set out in its accreditation standards. Several of the standards are directed at the investigation process and identify areas where campus safety personnel may have valuable expertise: securing the scene of an incident; providing for the safety of victims, alleged perpetrators, and witnesses; collecting evidence; or reporting the chronology of the incident. In particular, campus safety officers working with student affairs administrators can play an important role ensuring that student misconduct incidents that campus police discover result in timely referrals to the student disciplinary system for investigation.

In addition to making timely referrals of student incidents that violate campus policies and regulations to the appropriate student affairs or academic administrators (for example, the Title IX Coordinator or academic dean), coordination with campus safety departments regarding student misconduct investigations can be helpful in matters such as victim assistance, witness interviews, and securing property and evidence. Internal student misconduct investigations that involve weapons, illegal drugs, or sensitive documents can present unique issues for administrators unfamiliar with such items or lacking the facilities to securely store such evidence. Campus police departments may also aid in the preservation and storage of photographs, videotapes, and audio-recordings that often require special care or oversight. Moreover, campus police officers may have well-defined procedures in place to execute a verifiable chain-of-custody that could prevent tampering or otherwise place evidence in jeopardy. Working together with campus safety officers, colleges and universities can strengthen their internal investigation activities and standards while taking pragmatic steps to refute questions that attempt to cast doubt on the integrity of any internal investigation.

Reporting the Investigation Results and Findings

The purpose of the internal investigation is to encourage sound decision-making and reach a resolution at its conclusion. Or, perhaps better said, provide decision-makers with the best information available regarding matters that pose a threat to the institution, and students in particular. This effort will most readily be achieved through the fact-finding function of the investigation; however, the results of an internal investigation can provide potential legal conclusions and/or recommendations that may allow for the implementation of disciplinary action that corrects student conduct and minimizes the recurrence of behavior detrimental to persons within and connected to the academic community.

The substantive outcome of an internal investigation is obviously significant, but important consideration should be given to the methods used to present or deliver the investigation results and the consequences of each option. The traditional approach relies on the drafting and submission of a written narrative prepared by the investigator or investigative team that is understood as "the report." A written report offered at the close of an internal investigation is a predictable, common approach to sharing the results of an investigation that is, at the very least, reasonable. However, this traditional method of reporting an investigation's findings can have negative consequences. Because of the range of disclosure that may flow from a written internal investigation report involving a student misconduct incident, campus officials should take into consideration the likely reactions triggered by the publication and disclosure of a written investigation report.

That said, an investigation of student behavior almost by definition is a "hope for the best but plan for the worst" venture. Practical concern often relates to the number of variables or constituency groups that can become energized by a troublesome finding of student misconduct. Students, parents, faculty, alumni, trustees, politicians, and the media can all become a demanding force in the wake of an unfavorable published report. But this phase of the investigation process should not place campus leaders, student affairs personnel, or executive decision-makers in a "wait and see" posture. Put another way, an internal investigation need not sequester the investigation team in an operating room examining witnesses, evidence, and documents while the campus administration is compelled to take refuge in a holding room waiting to learn the plight of its students, employees, or institution's credibility. Once an investigation has commenced, tentative reports regarding the chronology of relevant events can be shared and updated during the course of the investigation, providing campus officials with important insight. Prior to a final report, investigators can also offer a tentative legal or compliance analysis identifying potential claims that may arise from the misconduct under investigation. With respect to both of these preliminary or tentative inquiries, campus administrators should be wary of interfering with the investigation or trampling on the investigator's independent ability to act.[15]

Beyond choosing to provide periodic reporting while the investigation is ongoing, there looms the decision as to whether the final report of an investigation should be a written or an oral report. This is a crucial decision that may impact multiple issues such as public disclosure of institutional blunders, negative publicity and its influence on key stakeholders, and potential legal charges from adversely affected parties. More specifically, deciding whether an internal investigation report should be a written report or an oral report is a question of priorities. On the one hand, the college or university may have a strong interest in protecting the conclusions of the investigation from public disclosure. On the other hand, the institution and its leadership may have an interest in documenting the investigation and presenting findings to demonstrate that it has been forthcoming and transparent regarding the incident at issue.[16]

An oral report that shares the results and findings of an internal investigation has certain advantages: (1) the findings of the investigation are more likely to remain confidential; (2) it is inherently difficult for critics to challenge the outcome of an investigation that is presented through an oral report; and (3) an oral report can be produced in a streamlined and inexpensive manner. Some courts have held that testimony related to an internal investigation is excludable where no written report was offered.[17] But a written report is often preferred because: (1) it demonstrates that a credible investigation has been conducted; and (2) allows all interested parties to examine the institution's actions, key facts, and evidence that justify any remedial or disciplinary actions.

In situations wherein the results of the internal investigation are captured in a written report and the drafters of the report are attorneys or acting through legal counsel, certain protections from public disclosure may be retained by indicating that the document is "privileged and confidential" or that the report is "prepared in anticipation for litigation." Otherwise, written reports that are disclosed to third parties, or subsequently used as an affirmative defense or evidence that the institution has met certain compliance obligations, may effectively waive any protection from disclosure.

It should also be noted that an internal investigation written report may draw the ire of individuals who believe they have been disparaged or wrongly criticized by the report. Persons mentioned in a report may assert claims for "defamation, invasion of privacy, publicity in a false light, tortious interference with economic interests, or for infliction of mental distress. *See Pearce v. E.F. Hutton, Inc.*, 664 F. Supp. 1490 (D.D.C. 1987) (former E.F. Hutton branch manager sued E.F. Hutton and former Attorney General Griffin Bell in connection with a report of an internal investigation that Griffin Bell had prepared on behalf of E.F. Hutton)."[18] For investigations conducted by campus administrators or student affairs personnel, it is reasonable to consider what posture the institution would take in the event allegations are made against parties responsible for conducting an internal investigation and preparing a final written report. Ideally, investigators would be protected or indemnified in the event they face charges for alleged investigatory misconduct. In sum, the manner in which the results of an internal investigation will be produced should not be taken for granted. Preemptive thinking, therefore, is a must not only during the investigative process, but also for determining how the outcome of the investigation will be communicated and what audiences may be given access to the investigation's findings.

Conclusion

An internal investigation is designed to assess the cause, scope, and frequency of wrongdoing or misconduct and the significance posed by any threat to an organization's mission. For postsecondary institutions of education, organizational threats can take various forms—financial instability, poor relationships with external audiences, breaches of campus safety, noncompliance with state or federal law, or public relations or media debacles, just to suggest a few. Student misconduct certainly can lead to campus unrest and conflict that can have a pervasive impact on the institution, thus justifying the need for policies and regulations to discipline or, if needed, even remove such students from the campus. However, student misconduct and the consequences that can flow from action taken by the institution can be detrimental to a student's future, and students know it.

It is vital that an institution's efforts to investigate and resolve student misconduct matters avoid being characterized as confrontational and that student affairs personnel not be viewed as the adversary. For those involved in the internal investigation process, this may be difficult to achieve because the investigator is viewed as the authority that determines right and wrong, the person or team of individuals who will decide what is truth or who is to blame. Rarely is a misconduct investigation viewed by students as anything other than a process that results in punishment. Although certain student misconduct may require sanctions or penalties, that possibility cannot be the dominant feature of any campus system designed to manage student affairs. Disciplinary and judicial procedures created to manage student behavioral misconduct should be, at the very least, influenced by the institution's educational mission. As for elements of the investigation process—the collection of facts, management of student interviews, and the articulation of findings and outcomes—these functions should take on a constructive and remedial form and not a prosecutorial or punitive tone. The focus of a student misconduct system should be on helping the student find his or her way back to the track that originally led the student to the college or university. Only when an institution's system determines that a student is no longer fit to matriculate toward degree completion should the disciplinary action and the effort to restore the student part ways.

The Design of Disciplinary Systems in Higher Education

Student misconduct or behavioral wrongdoing can range from modest incidents to emotionally disruptive behavior. Professors often are confronted with minor student misbehavior that can include texting during class lectures, eating in class, or causing unwanted distractions during lectures or small group exercises. Other more serious forms of student misconduct can involve emotional outbursts, physical threats, or rebellious actions that require a definitive response by the institution. In either case, what is required is that academic faculty, administrators, and members of the support staff operate or respond through a coherent system that leads to corrective action (figure 3).

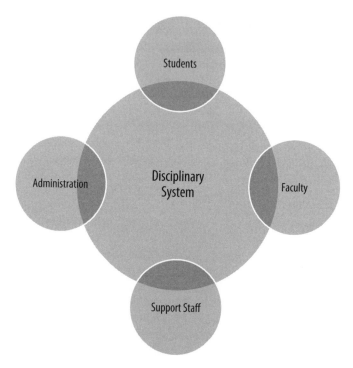

Figure 3. The Disciplinary System

Students should not be left in the dark about what conse-quences may result from their conduct and how the institution will proceed to consider what penalty, if any, may result from their actions. For the part of the college or university, faculty, administrators, and support staff must be trained to understand what the institution's disciplinary policies seek to achieve and their role in the process.[1] Faculty and student affairs personnel should have the skill to resolve student misconduct that involves minor infractions, like arriving late to class or using offensive language during class discussion, as well as misbehavior that es-calates to a campus safety threat, such as possessing a weapon or gun on campus.

The features and objectives of a student disciplinary system must fit the institution and reflect the values that are important to the university's mission. Every college or university has its own customs, traditions, and values that impact student affairs policy and practice. Some colleges may choose to utilize a *traditional honor system* that insists that students pledge to abide by certain behavioral standards, take personal responsibility for their own conduct, and even play a significant role in adjudication proceedings. Other universities may be more comfortable with a *modified honor system* that relies on faculty and the administration to execute the adjudication process, limiting the burden placed on students to deal with rule violations.[2] However, there are various other approaches that can be used to develop systems to resolve student misconduct.

Some institutions may decide to implement systems or schemes that separate student misconduct by the nature of the disciplinary matter. For example, academic wrongdoing, such as cheating on an exam or plagiarizing material, is distinguishable from non-academic misconduct that includes behavioral violations, such as substance abuse, sexual assault, or theft. Bifurcating student misconduct between academic and non-academic misconduct may have practical significance because the policies, rules, and personnel relied upon to resolve these forms of disputes may differ substantially at many institutions.[3] There may also be important ramifications for the investigation process. For instance, an allegation of cheating or plagiarism typically will require some investigation to review the materiality of any academic infraction. Who witnessed the cheating? What sources were improperly utilized in a written essay or student writing? Did the faculty member involved rush to judgment or provide poor guidance and supervision that contributed to the student's alleged academic misconduct? These are logical questions that an internal investigation by academic officials or persons designated by the provost or chief academic officer would be expected to explore.

On the other hand, incidents concerning non-academic misconduct may benefit from a disciplinary system that offers more discretion and flexibility. Non-academic complaints against students can involve *nuisance* matters like excessive talking on a cellphone in the library, socializing in the faculty lounge without permission, or something as immature as sleeping in class. These kinds of infractions are perhaps best left to informal intervention by faculty, counselors, or others who have the sensitivity and gravitas to impress upon students that their conduct matters and that even nuisance misconduct can put a student on the wrong path. An honor system might not be effective at managing this type of misconduct and could be viewed as using a proverbial sledge hammer to kill a fly.

Hence, a student misconduct disciplinary system can resolve disputes by accurately identifying wrongdoing but result in unjust outcomes that fuel the flames of distrust, fear, and confrontation among the student body. To avoid this situation, the disciplinary system may need to consider a reasonable balance between rigidity and informality.

Other non-academic infractions, especially incidents that pose a threat to campus safety or represent a clear violation of campus rules or regulations, require an administrative system that considers due process protections that students are entitled to as well as a process consistent with an institution's educational goals. Thus, the basic design of a student misconduct or disciplinary system can involve multiple stages that can include investigation, adjudication, and an appeals process. With regard to the investigation function, experienced student affairs administrators have observed that the role of the investigator should be carefully contemplated by campus policy-makers.

The Pre-adjudication Investigation Stage functions to complement the second stage, where all three tasks (fact finding, rule interpretation, and choice of sanction) are ordinarily accomplished at the Adjudication Meeting. In designing the Pre-adjudication Investigation Stage, campus planners must select one role from among several different roles that may be assigned to the pre-adjudication investigator. . . . They then design a role for the pre-adjudication investigator that will contribute to produce sound educational outcomes at the Pre-adjudication Stage as well as at the Adjudication Stage.[4]

The investigation function certainly should not be executed simply by intuition but through a deliberative process that examines what impact the investigation may have on students literally or their likely perceptions of the disciplinary process. Can an internal investigation lead to productive open dialogue between students and student affairs administrators? Or will it discourage students from coming forward with information or evidence they may have about an incident? What role might an investigator have in the early resolution of disputes or the adoption of reasonable sanctions? Also, an investigation that is expected to critique and, if possible, reveal the underlying causes for behavioral misconduct, honor code violations, or academic dishonesty can have tremendous value for the college or university developing future student personnel policy. That is, assuming the investigation effort has the support, resources, and time to conduct a probing inquiry regarding the alleged academic or non-academic misconduct.

Furthermore, the design of any student disciplinary system must be inclusive of procedures and protocols that insist upon objectivity and fairness throughout the process, including the investigatory phase of a student misconduct inquiry. Disciplinary systems that are created to assess student misconduct should expect to be scrutinized, and where the investigation process can be shown to have been prejudicial, any action that relied on the investigation's findings would be called into question. More importantly, the presence of a fair and equitable student misconduct investigation process serves a "greater good" that promotes values such as honesty, fair play, and truthfulness that all members of the higher education community should acknowledge.

The Evolving Role of the Student Affairs Practitioner

The work of student affairs personnel is perhaps more challenging and diverse than ever. While the tasks of managing residence halls, advising students academically, and counseling student organizations continue as some of the mainstay functions, student affairs administrators also must be capable of supporting a range of topics that can include diversity initiatives, campus safety, and students who may have learning challenges. Moreover, colleges and universities occupy a unique position in American society, garnering attention from students and the general public because of the popularity of college sports and other attractions that universities can support, such an a venue for entertainment or outlet for public services. Just consider the thousands of people who visit colleges across the country each year for a concert, play, or sports event, or the many children whose first visit to a university is for a summer camp program. The increased attention and growing sophistication of American life has certainly spilled over into college life and the work of student affairs.

For some, the work of student affairs administration has grown too demanding relative to the rewards and compensation available for entry-level positions. Studies conducted regarding the career development of student affairs professionals have warned that notable attrition rates triggered by concerns about long working hours and the lack of upward mobility to senior positions may have an impact on the talent pool available to fill this segment of the higher education workforce.[5] Thus as the volume of student misconduct incidents becomes increasingly complex, the dearth of highly motivated and trained student affairs personnel may emerge as a difficult reality for some institutions in the future.

In light of this challenge, the obvious question for the higher education community is whether the student affairs practitioner has grown to meet the needs of the institution and the students on our campuses. The easy answer is that there is work to be done elevating the status and support provided to student affairs professionals, especially those charged with investigating and resolving student misconduct matters. Of course, no two campuses are the same and student affairs personnel at many institutions are well prepared to perform their duties. However, an ongoing review process and internal assessment of staff capabilities, training needs, professional satisfaction, and institutional commitment is vital to ensuring that student affairs personnel are well equipped to serve a diverse student population.

Indemnification for Student Affairs Professionals

The outcome of a student misconduct investigation is rarely, if ever, predictable, but what does linger throughout the course of any investigation is the possibility that a student might be burdened with disciplinary action. Besides suffering the disappointment that may ensue from an adverse disciplinary decision that results in academic dismissal or some other form of sanction, students, with the insistence of their families and friends, may also seek retribution against the institution and student affairs personnel involved in any investigation that supported the disciplinary action. This can even result in legal action or lawsuits wherein university officials are named as individual defendants and charged with particular wrongdoing.

For student affairs administrators and other employees engaged to conduct internal investigations, it is wise that the institution's commitment related to providing a legal defense, indemnification, and liability protection in the form of insurance for investigators be well-defined prior to any reactionary claims raised by students. As a general matter, administrators acting within the scope of their job duties should expect protection or indemnification by their institution even when they are individually named in a lawsuit. A college or university may have policies, practices, or other obligations to indemnify employees or administrators who are individually sued for actions taken within the course of performing their job duties. However, such indemnification may become void where it is evident that the administrator acted illegally or outside the scope of his or her job duties. Also, action by the college or university to indemnify or pay an employee's legal expenses should not be coerced or extended as a tradeoff for investigators to influence their decision-making or actions during the investigation. To do so would clearly compromise the integrity of any student misconduct investigation and at a minimum tarnish the institution's reputation as a good faith actor.

Finally, a goal of this book has been to consider the investigation of student misconduct in the context of the legal and strategic hurdles that influence sound administrative action and to offer some guidance for higher education decision-makers to respond. With this goal in mind, what should not be lost is the reality that the student misconduct investigation is an opportunity to manage risk. By implementing efficient, impartial, thorough investigative processes where student conduct exposes the campus community to harm, danger, or other forms of mayhem, colleges and universities have a golden opportunity to stave off the consequences of student misconduct. *A laudable goal indeed.*

Notes

Introduction

1. Moore v. Student Affairs Comm. of Troy State Univ., 284 F. Supp. 725, 729 (M.D. Ala. 1968).

2. Jack New, *States Requiring Colleges to Note Sexual Assault Responsibility on Student Transcript*, INSIDE HIGHER ED, July 10, 2015, https://insidehighered.com/news/2015/07/10/states-requiring-colleges-note-sexual-assault-responsibility-student-transcripts; and Samantha Cooney, *Bill Would Require Colleges to Put Sexual Assault Record on Transcripts*, TIME, December 9, 2016, http://time.com/4596813/sexual-assault-transcripts-bill/.

3. Sarah Helene Duggin, *Internal Corporate Investigations: Legal Ethics, Professionalism, and the Employee Interview*, COLUM. BUS. L. REV., 2003, 859.

4. *2 Oklahoma Students Expelled over Racial Chant; House Mom Filmed Singing N-Word.* CNN WIRE (March 10, 2015), http://wtvr.com/2015/03/10/university-of-oklahoma-expels-two-students-over-racist-chant/; Alejandro Danois, *Inside Oklahoma's Healing Process in the Aftermath of the SAE Racism Scandal*, Special to BLEACHER REPORT (July 21, 2015), http://bleacherreport.com/articles/2512205-inside-oklahomas-healing-process-in-the-aftermath-of-the-sae-racism-scandal (discusses decision by the University of Oklahoma in more detail).

5. Thomas R. Baker, *Criminal Sanctions for Student Misconduct: Double Jeopardy Litigation in the 1990's*, 130 ED. LAW REP., 1, 15 (1998) (observing the role of student development principles in student disciplinary matters); Rachelle Winkle-Wagner, *Self, College Experiences, and Society: Rethinking the Theoretical Foundations of Student Development Theory*, 30 COLL. STUDENT AFF. J., 2 (2012), 45-60; Elizabeth M.

Baldizan, *Development, Due Process, and Reduction: Student Conduct in the 1990s*, NEW DIR. STUDENT SERV., 82 (Summer 1998): 29-37.

6. During the course of an investigation, numerous facts will be discovered. Significant attention should be given to those facts that satisfy the materiality threshold. *Material* is defined as "of such a nature that knowledge of the item would affect a person's decision-making." BLACK'S LAW DICTIONARY (10th ed. 2014).

7. Duff Wilson and David Barstow, *All Charges Dropped in Duke Case*, N. Y. TIMES, April 12, 2007, http://www.nytimes.com/2007/04/12/us/12duke.html?pagewanted=all.

8. Mark P. Goodman and Daniel J. Fetterman, *Defining the Objectives and Scope of an Investigation*, § 3:7 in DEFENDING CORPORATIONS AND INDIVIDUALS IN GOVERNMENT INVESTIGATIONS, December 2017 Update.

9. K. E. Weick, *Educational Organizations as Loosely Coupled Systems*, ADMIN. SCI. Q., 21 (1976), 1-19.

10. Laura L. Dunn, *Addressing Sexual Violence in Higher Education: Ensuring Compliance with the Clery Act, Title IX and Vawa*, 15 GEO. J. GENDER & L. 563, 578 (2014) (discussing the procedures used to effectively investigate student misconduct, emphasizing campus safety and complying with federal law); Matthew R. Triplett, *Sexual Assault on College Campuses: Seeking the Appropriate Balance between Due Process and Victim Protection*, 62 DUKE L.J. 487, 491-92 (2012) (explores the constitutional, statutory, and related concerns that comprise the legal environment that impacts sexual assault).

Chapter 1. Constitutional Considerations and Student Rights

1. For an unfortunate real-life example of how issues of racial bigotry can bring tragedy to a college community, see the following: Chris Quintana, *Black Student's Stabbing Death at U. of Maryland Is Being Investigated as a Hate Crime*, CHRON. HIGHER ED., MAY 22, 2017, http://www.chronicle.com/blogs/ticker/black-students-stabbing-death-at-u-of-maryland-is-being-investigated-as-a-hate-crime/118544.

2. Sweezy v. New Hampshire, 354 U.S. 234, 77 S. Ct. 1203, 1 L. Ed. 2d 1311 (1957). See Justice Frankfurter's concurrence in this classic US Supreme Court decision focused largely on academic freedom.

3. Shelton v. Tucker, 364 U.S. 479, 81 S. Ct. 247, 5 L. Ed. 2d 231 (1960).

4. Keyishian v. Bd. of Regents of Univ. of State of N. Y., 385 U.S. 589, 603, 87 S. Ct. 675, 683, 17 L. Ed.2d 629 (1967).

5. Steven Lee Myers, *Student Opens Fire at U. of Iowa, Killing 4 Before Shooting Himself,* N. Y. TIMES, November 2, 1991, http://www.nytimes .com/1991/11/02/us/student-opens-fire-at-u-of-iowa-killing-4-before -shooting-himself.html.

6. Allie Bice, *85 Ohio State Vet Students Caught in Test-Cheating Scandal,* USA TODAY COLL., June 12, 2016, http://college.usatoday.com/2016/06 /12/85-ohio-state-vet-students-caught-in-test-cheating-scandal/.

7. Dixon v. Alabama State Bd. of Ed., 294 F.2d 150, 157 (5th Cir. 1961).

8. Keefe v. Adams, 840 F.3d 523, 534 (8th Cir. 2016).

9. *Dixon,* 294 F.2d at 152, note 3 (emphasis added).

10. Benedict P. Kuehne, *Protecting the Privilege in the Corporate Setting: Conducting and Defending Internal Corporate Investigations,* 9 ST. THOMAS L. REV. 651, 664 (1997) (borrowing from the corporate context, not every incident will require an internal investigation, but misdeeds should be detected as early as possible to limit future exposure).

11. Edmund Donnelly, *What Happens When Student-Athletes Are the Ones Who Blow the Whistle?: How* Lowery v. Euverard *Exposes a Deficiency in the First Amendment Rights of Student-Athletes,* 43 NEW ENG. L. REV. 943, 959–60 (2009) (discussing the various legal whistleblower protections granted by the state and federal governments nationwide and why the conduct of student whistleblowers may be beneficial to society).

12. Frank D. LoMonte, *"The Key Word Is Student": Hazelwood Censorship Crashes the Ivy-Covered Gates,* 11 FIRST AMEND. L. REV. 305, 363 (2013) (referring to a student complaint regarding the nursing school grading system that could have been viewed as constitutionally protected speech of a whistleblower).

13. *Student Who Exposed Cruelty Urges Others to Act,* NURSING STANDARD 28, no. 30 (March 26, 2014); *Student Whistleblowers Need Legal Safeguards, Says RCN,* NURSING STANDARD, 27, no. 28 (March 13, 2013). Also see, Note, *Blown Coverage: Tackling the Law's Failure to Protect Athlete-Whistleblowers,* 14 VA. SPORTS & ENT. L.J. 250, no.2 (Spring 2015), which examines retaliation protections for student-athletes who act as whistleblowers by exposing misconduct by coaches.

14. Don Troop, *California Court Says College Students Cannot Expect Protection from Classroom Crimes,* CHRON. HIGHER ED., October 8, 2015, http://chronicle.com/blogs/ticker/california-court-says-college -students-cannot-expect-protection-from-classroom-crimes/105715.

15. Nick DeSantis, *American U. Investigates Underground Fraternity Emails That Sparked Uproar,* CHRON. HIGHER ED., April 23, 2014, http:// chronicle.com/blogs/ticker/jp/american-u-investigates-underground -fraternity-emails-that-sparked-an-uproar.

16. *Theft Accusations Spur Kentucky State U. to Suspend 13 Female Basketball Players,* CHRON. HIGHER ED., November 15, 1999, http://chronicle .com/article/Theft-Accusations-Spur/111958.

17. John J. Copelan, Jr., and Barbara S. Monahan, *Preventive Law: A Strategy for Local Governments in the Nineties,* 44 SYRACUSE L. REV. 957, 958 (1993).

18. Preventive Law is not a drastic or radically different approach to law practice but redirects the focus from litigation to risk management. Z. Jill Barclift, *Preventive Law: A Strategy for Internal Corporate Lawyers to Advise Managers of Their Ethical Obligations,* 33 J. LEGAL PROF. 31, 34 (2008).

19. Waliga v. Board of Trustees of Kent State University, 488 N.E. 2d 850, 852–853 (Ohio 1986) (noting that a university has the power to revoke degrees).

20. *Fiduciary Duties of College and University Faculty and Administrators,* 29 J.C. & U.L. 153, 162 (2002).

21. Belk v. Chancellor of Washington Univ., 336 F. Supp. 45, 46 (E.D. Mo. 1970) (observing that "it is axiomatic that the due process provision of the Fourteenth Amendment to the United States Constitution upon which this cause of action is based encompasses only 'state action,' and that the acts of private individuals will not be considered unless they are acting under color of state law. Shelley v. Kraemer, 334 U.S. 1, 68 S. Ct. 836, 92 L. Ed. 1161 (1948); Evans v. Newton, 382 U.S. 296, 86 S. Ct. 486, 15 L. Ed.2d 373 (1966)").

22. *Caleb,* 598 Fed Appx. at 235.

23. Howard Gillman and Erwin Chemerinsky, *Don't Mock or Ignore Students' Lack of Support for Free Speech. Teach Them,* L.A. TIMES, Op-Ed, March 31, 2016, http://www.latimes.com/opinion/op-ed/la-oe -chemerinsky-gillman-free-speech-on-campus-20160331-story.html.

24. Osei v. Temple Univ., 2011 U.S. Dist. LEXIS 113431 (E.D. Pa. Sept. 30, 2011) (finding that a student threatening to shoot a counselor was not speech protected by the First Amendment).

25. Virginia v. Black, 538 U.S. 343, 359–60, 123 S. Ct. 1536, 1548, 155 L. Ed.2d 535 (2003).

26. Emily Tate, *Diving into Diversity and Safe Spaces,* INSIDE HIGHER ED., March 13, 2017, https://www.insidehighered.com/news/2017/03/13 /ace-panel-discusses-diversity-and-safe-spaces-campus (ACE panel discussion by campus leaders about free expression and inclusion).

27. See John H. Dunkle et al., *Managing Violent and Other Troubling Students: The Role of Threat Assessment Teams on Campus*, 34 J.C. & U.L., 585, 589 (2008) (providing a discussion regarding traditional concepts of threat assessment).

28. Cornelius v. NAACP Legal Def. & Educ. Fund, Inc., 473 U.S. 788, 815, 105 S. Ct. 3439, 3455, 87 L. Ed.2d 567 (1985).

29. *Id.* at 801.

30. Tinker v. Des Moines Indep. Cmty. Sch Dist., 393 U.S. 503, 504, 89 S. Ct. 733, 735, 21 L. Ed. 2d 731 (1969). K.A. ex rel. Ayers v. Pocono Mountain Sch. Dist., 710 F.3d 99, 106 (3d Cir. 2013).

31. *Keefe,* 840 F.3d, at 529.

32. *Id.* at 531.

33. Marshall v. Indiana Univ., 170 F. Supp. 3d 1201, 1209 (S.D. Ind. 2016).

34. Peter Schmidt, *Women's Groups Urge Colleges and Government to Rein in Yik Yak,* CHRON. HIGHER ED., May 21, 2015, http://chronicle.com /article/Women-s-Groups-Urge-Colleges/233864.

35. Also, it should be noted that legislation has been introduced in Congress to protect students against demands by educational institutions for access to social media outlets maintained by students under the Social Networking Online Protection Act (SNOPA), which prohibits educational institutions from requiring that students grant access to their social media accounts. See Hillary Gunther, *Employment, College Students & Social Media, a Recipe for Disaster: Why the Proposed Social Networking Online Protection Act Is Not Your Best Facebook "Friend,"* 24 ALB. L.J. SCI. & TECH. 515, 516 (2014).

36. Katherine Knott, *Students at UPenn Protest Email as Evidence of Rape Culture,* CHRON. HIGHER ED., September 7, 2016, http://www

.chronicle.com/blogs/ticker/students-plaster-hundreds-this-is-what
-rape-culture-looks-like-fliers-around-u-of-pennslyvania/114062.

37. 410 Fed. Appx. 134 (10th Cir. 2011).

38. *Id.* at 134, 135.

39. Esteban v. Central Missouri State College, 415 F.2d 1077, 1088 (1969) (discussing campus regulations designed to address student conduct without having a chilling effect on constitutional rights).

40. O'Connor v. Ortega, 480 U.S. 709, 107 S. Ct. 1492, 94 L. Ed.2d 714 (1987) (examining an employer's authority to conduct a workplace search); New Jersey v. T.L.O., 469 U.S. 325, 334, 105 S. Ct. 733, 83 L. Ed.2d 720 (1985) (discussing the conditions under which public school officials may search a student).

41. "[P]ublic employees' expectations of privacy in their offices, desks, and file cabinets, like similar expectations of employees in the private sector, may be reduced by virtue of actual office practices and procedures, or by legitimate regulation." *O'Connor,* at 717, 107 S. Ct. 1492. See also Wasson v. Sonoma Cty. Jr. Coll. Dist., 4 F. Supp. 2d 893, 905 (N.D. Cal. 1997), *aff'd on other grounds sub nom*, and Wasson v. Sonoma Cty. Junior Coll., 203 F.3d 659 (9th Cir. 2000).

42. US Constitution, Fifth Amendment.

43. *Fifth Amendment at Trial,* 44 GEO. L.J. ANN. REV. CRIM. PROC. 707 (2015).

44. Nzuve v. Castleton State Coll. acknowledged that a leading case on the subject matter, Goldberg v. Regents of University of California, 248 Cal. App. 2d 867, 57 Cal. Rptr. 463 (1967), squarely held that discipline imposed by the academic community need not await the outcome of other proceedings.

45. *Nzuve,* 133 Vt. at 231; Hart v. Ferris State College, 557 F. Supp. 1379, 1384–85 (W.D. Mich. 1983); Grossner v. Columbia University, 287 F. Supp. 535 (S.D.N.Y. 1968).

46. Goldberg v. Regents of Univ. of Cal.

47. *Id.* at 462, 472.

48. Hart v. Ferris State College, 557 F. Supp. 1379, 1384 (W.D. Mich. 1983) (discussing the application of the US Supreme Court decision in *Garrity* in a student misconduct matter).

49. Goss v. Lopez, 419 U.S. 565, 95 S. Ct. 729, 42 L. Ed. 2d 725 (1975); Dixon v. Alabama State Board of Education, 294 F.2d 150, cert denied, 368 U.S. 930, 82 S. Ct. 368, 7 L. Ed.2d 193 (1961). These cases discuss

the purview of the due process in public education and rights available to students facing misconduct allegations at public colleges and universities.

50. *Hart,* 557 at 1385. See Robert J. Goodwin, *The Fifth Amendment in Public Schools: A Rationale for Its Application in Investigations and Disciplinary Proceedings,* 28 WM. & MARY L. REV. 683, 708 (1987).

51. *Guse,* 2011 WL 1256727, *12.

52. *Id.,* 12-13.

53. This popular 1990 dramatic action movie adapted from a Tom Clancy novel provides a great example of just how badly things can go wrong when the stakes are really high and desperation drives the search for an answer.

54. A limitation to this tactical approach would involve the inability to guarantee confidentiality. Campus officials may be compelled to provide information produced during an investigation through discovery or a court order.

Chapter 2. Statutory Law and Avoiding Investigatory Mishaps

1. The relevant portion of FERPA reads: "No funds shall be made available under any applicable program to any educational agency or institution which has a policy or practice of permitting the release of education records (or personally identifiable information contained therein other than directory information, as defined in paragraph (5) of subsection (a) of this section) of students without the written consent of their parents to any individual, agency, or organization." 20 U.S.C. § 1232g(b)(1).

2. FERPA specifies that "sensitive information about students *may not be released* without [the student's] consent." United States v. Miami Univ., 294 F.3d 797, 806-07 (6th Cir. 2002); and, Owasso Independent School District v. Falvo, 534 U.S. 426, 122 S. Ct. 934, 937, 151 L. Ed.2d 896 (2002).

3. Unincorporated Operating Div. of Indiana Newspapers, Inc. v. Trustees of Indiana Univ., 787 N.E.2d 893, 904 (Ind. Ct. App. 2003) (wherein news outlets sought student educational records in connection with an investigation).

4. 34 C.F.R. § 99.31 (a)(9).

5. Courts have recognized that the US Department of Education issued guidance on this potential conflict between FERPA and Title IX. In

Bigge v. Dist. Sch. Bd. of Citrus Cty., Fla., No. 5:11-CV-210-OC-10TBS, 2011 WL 6002927, at *2 (M.D. Fla. Nov. 28, 2011), the court stated that FERPA is part of the General Education Provisions Act (GEPA), 20 U.S.C. § 1221. GEPA states that "[n]othing in this chapter shall be construed to affect the applicability of . . . Title IX of the Education Amendments of 1972." 20 U.S.C. § 1221(d). The US Department of Education has interpreted this provision to mean that "if there is a direct conflict between the requirements of FERPA and the requirements of Title IX, such that enforcement of FERPA would interfere with the primary purpose of Title IX to eliminate sex-based discrimination in schools, the requirements of Title IX override any conflicting FERPA provisions." U.S. Department of Education Revised Sexual Harassment Guidance at vii (2001).

However, notwithstanding the DOE's guidance it is helpful to know that on occasion courts may be forced to balance student privacy interests against the need to order disclosure of information. See also Brian A. Pappas, *Out from the Shadows: Title IX, University Ombuds, and the Reporting of Campus Sexual Misconduct*, 94 DENV. U. L. REV. 71, 88 (2016).

6. 34 C.F.R. § 99.31 (a)(13).
7. Robert M. Goerge, *Barriers to Accessing State Data and Approaches to Addressing Them*, 675 ANNALS AM. ACAD. POL. & SOC. SCI. 122, 137 (2018).
8. Matthew R. Salzwedel and Jon Ericson, *Cleaning Up Buckley: How the Family Educational Rights and Privacy Act Shields Academic Corruption in College Athletics*, 2003 WIS. L. REV. 1053, 1075-77 (2003).
9. See Letter from LeRoy S. Rooker, Family Policy Compliance Office, FPCO Director, to Shelton State Community College (Aug. 7, 1998).
10. *Id.* at (a)(1).
11. Daryl J. Lapp, Esq., *Student Privacy Issues,* Massachusetts Continuing Legal Education, Inc., CULM MA-CLE 4-1. See Letter from LeRoy S. Rooker, Director, Family Policy Compliance Office, US Department of Education, to Dr. Peter Likens, President, University of Arizona (March 11, 1999) (https://www2.ed.gov/policy/gen/guid/fpco/ferpa /library/Shelton_al.html). See also Elana Zeide, *Student Privacy Principles for the Age of Big Data: Moving Beyond FERPA and FIPPS*, 8 DREXEL L. REV. 339, 364 (2016), which states that "most institutions

define 'legitimate educational interest' in terms of functionality rather than substantive criteria."

12. Jun Yu v. Idaho State Univ., No. 4:15-CV-00430-REB, 2017 WL 1158813, at *2 (D. Idaho Mar. 27, 2017) (FERPA does not provide a "privilege" that prevents disclosure of student records but seeks to deter the adoption of school policies for releasing student records).

13. *Id.* at *3.

14. The Crime Awareness and Campus Security Act of 1990 is a subpart of the Student Right-to-Know and Campus Security Act, Pub. L. 101-542, Title II 104 Stat. 2581, 2384-2387. The Clery Act amended the Higher Education Act of 1965 by § 485(f), 20 U.S.C. § 1092(f) and requires that colleges and universities report and disclose campus crime statistics and comply with campus safety and security provisions as mandated by the Title IV and other Higher Education Act programs. The law is enforced by the US Department of Education and applies to public and private institutions participating in the federal student financial aid programs.

15. Pub. L. 113-4, Title III, §304(a), March 7, 2013, 127 Stat. 89.

16. 20 U.S.C. §1092 (f)(1)(F)(iii).

17. It is also useful to note that Title VI of the Civil Rights Act, 42 U.S.C. § 2000d, which prohibits discrimination on account of race, color, or national origin in all programs and activities receiving federal financial assistance, can also trigger the need for an internal investigation. In Sirpal v. Univ. of Miami, 684 F. Supp. 2d 1349, 1358-1359 (S.D. Fla. 2010), a graduate student was able to state a cognizable claim under Title VI related to his dismissal from a PhD program and suspension from medical school where university officials failed to conduct an independent investigation to support their decision but rather relied in part on a decision-maker who may have acted with discriminatory intent. See also Matthew D. O'Neill, *Searching for Enforcement: Title VI Regulations and Section 1983*, 61 U. KAN. L. REV. 787, 793 (2013), which discusses the similarities between Title VI and Title IX.

18. United States Statutes at Large, Declaration of Independence, 44 Stat. 1845 and Gettysburg Address, Abraham Lincoln, November 19, 1863, http://teachingamericanhistory.org/library/document/gettysburg -address/.

19. The US Supreme Court's decision in Brown v. Board of Ed. of Topeka, Shawnee Cty., Kan., 347 U.S. 483, 74 S. Ct. 686, 98 L. Ed. 873 (1954), supplemented sub nom. Brown v. Bd. of Ed. of Topeka, Kan., 349 U.S. 294, 75 S. Ct. 753, 99 L. Ed. 1083 (1955), rejected the separate but equal doctrine and paved the way for racial desegregation in public accommodation, housing, education, and numerous facets of American life. In addition to passing the 1964 Civil Rights Act, Congress passed the Voting Rights Act of 1965, which sought to prevent acts of discrimination at the state and local levels where African Americans were systematically denied the right to vote as protected by the Fifteenth Amendment to the US Constitution.

20. Paul M. Anderson, *Title IX at Forty: An Introduction and Historical Review of Forty Legal Developments That Shaped Gender Equity Law,* 22 MARQ. SPORTS L. REV. 325, 326 (2012) (providing a historical overview of Title IX).

21. The US Department of Education describes guidance documents on its website as follows: "Guidance documents represent the Department of Education's (ED) current thinking on a topic. They do not create or confer any rights for or on any person and do not impose any requirements beyond those required under applicable law and regulations." http://www2.ed.gov/policy/gen/guid/types-of-guidance-documents.html (last viewed June 20, 2016). Moreover, it should be understood that courts have indicated that "Dear Colleague Letters" and "Questions and Answers" guidance, when used as authoritative documents regarding whether a plaintiff has alleged a plausible Title IX claim, do not carry the force of law and are not entitled to *Chevron* deference because they were not promulgated pursuant to notice-and-comment rulemaking. Farmer v. Kansas State Univ., No. 16-CV-2256-JAR-GEB, 2017 WL 980460, at *6 (D. Kan. Mar. 14, 2017). In addition, it is worth noting that OCR may amend or withdraw statements of policy and guidance documents when it deems such action necessary. See https://www2.ed.gov/about/offices/list/ocr/letters/colleague-title-ix-201709.pdf (last visited November 22, 2017) stating OCR's withdrawal of the following: OCR, "Dear Colleague Letter on Sexual Violence," from the US Department of Education regarding Title IX requirements and efforts to prevent sexual harassment and sexual violence and educate students and employees, April 4, 2011, http://www2.ed.gov/about/offices/list/ocr

/letters/colleague-201104.pdf; and OCR, "Questions and Answers on Title IX and Sexual Violence," April 29, 2014, http://www2.ed.gov /about/offices/list/ocr/docs/qa-201404-title-ix.pdf.

22. OCR, *Revised Sexual Harassment Guidance: Harassment of Students by School Employees, Other Students, or Third Parties*, January 2001, http://www2.ed.gov/about/offices/list/ocr/docs/shguide.pdf. OCR, "Dear Colleague Letter" from the US Department of Education concerning recipients' obligations to protect students from student-on-student harassment, which clarifies the relationship between bullying and discriminatory harassment and how a school should respond to such misconduct, October 26, 2010, http://www2.ed.gov /about/offices/list/ocr/letters/colleague-201010.pdf. OCR, "Dear Colleague Letter," from the US Department of Education regarding the prohibition against retaliation under federal civil rights laws. The DCL confirms OCR's enforcement authority and discusses the basic principles of retaliation law, April 24 2013, http://www2.ed.gov/about /offices/list/ocr/letters/colleague-201304.pdf. OCR, "Dear Colleague Letter," regarding key issues with respect to a Title IX Coordinator, April 24, 2015, http://www2.ed.gov/about/offices/list/ocr/letters /colleague-201504-title-ix-coordinators.pdf.

23. Dear Colleague Letter withdrawing OCR guidance, at https://www .cmu.edu/title-ix/colleague-title-ix-201709.pdf .

24. As mentioned above, the 2014 guidance has been withdrawn.

25. *Fundamentals of Investigating and Interviewing*, GPSOLO, July/ August 2014, at 26, 30–31 (conflicts checks should be run as new information is gathered and new witnesses are identified as part of an investigation to avoid ethical dilemmas); Sarah H. Duggin, "Ethical Challenges of Internal Investigations," in *Clean Water Act: Law and Regulation* (ALI-ABA Course of Study, SM020, American Law Institute, Philadelphia, 2006), p. 319 at 325 (pre-investigation conflicts checks should include review for representation of constituents of client entity and third parties who may be involved in investigation).

26. See also Thomas v. Univ. of Pittsburgh, No. CIV.A. 13-514, 2014 WL 3055361, at *7–8 (W.D. Pa. July 3, 2014).

27. *Doe v. Brown Univ.*, 210 F. Supp. 3d 310, 316–17 (D.R.I. 2016).

28. See the discussion in chapter 1 regarding constitutional protections under the Fifth and Fourteenth Amendments.

29. See *Not Alone,* the first report of the White House Task Force to Protect Students from Sexual Assault, https://www.notalone.gov/assets/report.pdf (last viewed June 21, 2016).

30. See "Dear Colleague Letter" on Title IX Coordinators at http://www2.ed.gov/about/offices/list/ocr/letters/colleague-201504-title-ix-coordinators.pdf (last viewed June 21, 2016).

31. See *Q&A on Campus Sexual Misconduct,* September 2017 at https://www2.ed.gov/about/offices/list/ocr/docs/qa-title-ix-201709.pdf (last viewed November 22, 2017).

32. For an excellent discussion regarding Title IX see Peter Lake's book *The Four Corners of Title IX Regulatory Compliance: A Primer for American Colleges and Universities,* at http://hierophantenterprises.com/.

33. *Fiduciary Duties of College and University Faculty and Administrators,* 29 J.C. & U.L. 153, 154 (2002) (discussing the fiduciary obligations colleges and universities owe students who rely on faculty and administrators in pursuing their education).

34. Marta McLaughlin, "Shifting the Burden? The Best of Intentions—The Toll of Conviction at Any Cost," 27 AM. J. CRIM. L. 439, 441 (2000) (book review of *Mean Justice* by Edward Humes discussing investigatory misconduct and reliance on misinformation obtained from unreliable interviews in a criminal law context).

35. Seth F. Kreimer, *Pervasive Image Capture and the First Amendment: Memory, Discourse, and the Right to Record,* 159 U. PA. L. REV. 335, 358 (2011) (acknowledging state statutes designed to regulate wiretapping and recording of oral communications absent the consent of all parties to the conversation). Diane Leenheer Zimmerman, *I Spy: The Newsgatherer Under Cover,* 33 U. RICH. L. REV. 1185, 1215, 1216 & n.139, 1217 (2000) (discussing states requiring the consent of parties in order to record conversation).

36. Erica Pearson and John Lauinger, *Hofstra Gang Rape Story Was All a Lie,* N.Y. DAILY NEWS, Sept. 17, 2009. Four men charged in the rape of a Hofstra University student were released from jail when a video recording made on a cellphone revealed the sex was consensual. However, it should be noted that in states where third-party surreptitious recordings are prohibited, a court may have suppressed and not considered the video recording.

37. Cassandra Feeney, *Are You "In Good Hands"?: Balancing Protection for Insurers and Insured in First-Party Bad-Faith Claims with a Uniform*

Standard, 45 NEW ENG. L. REV. 685, 708–09 (2011) (includes extreme examples of investigation misconduct by an insurance company).

38. Bruce A. Green and Ellen S. Podgor, *Unregulated Internal Investigations: Achieving Fairness for Corporate Constituents,* 54 B.C. L. REV. 73, 119 (2013).

Chapter 3. Fundamentals

1. See also Nick DeSantis, *2 Students at Miami U. Are Dismissed for Tampering with Grades,* CHRON. HIGHER ED., March 26, 2013, http://www.chronicle.com/blogs/ticker/2-students-at-miami-u-are -dismissed-for-tampering-with-grades/57561.

2. *General Order on Judicial Standards of Procedure and Substance in Review of Student Discipline in Tax-Supported Institutions of Higher Education,* 45 F.R.D. 133 (1968, 1969); David E. Morrison, *The Legality of University-Conducted Dormitory Searches for Internal Disciplinary Purposes,* DUKE L.J. 770–88 (1976) (discussing a college's inherent power to promulgate rules and regulations for student disciplinary purposes as acknowledged by the Supreme Court in Healy v. James, 408 U.S. 169 (1972)).

3. *Internal Investigations, Government Investigations, Whistleblower Concerns: Techniques to Protect Your Health Care Organization,* 51 ALA. L. REV. 205, 210 (1999) (observing the importance of the subject matter under investigation as well as to whom the investigative team will be accountable within the client organization).

4. Lee Gardner, *What's the Best Way to Lead After a Racial Incident on Campus,* CHRON. HIGHER ED., February 19, 2016, http://chronicle .com/article/What-s-the-Best-Way-to-Lead/235371?cid=trend_right_h) (discussing an incident at Texas A&M that is the subject of two investigations, one by the campus police and one by the student disciplinary council).

5. Casey McGowan, *The Threat of Expulsion as Unacceptable Coercion: Title IX, Due Process, and Coerced Confessions,* 66 EMORY L.J. 1175, 1185 (2017) (identifying three models that most colleges and universities use in Title IX matters).

6. Sarah Brown and Karin Fischer, *For Study-Abroad Offices, Sexual-Assault Cases May Be Unfamiliar Territory,* CHRON. HIGHER ED., November 23, 2015, http://www.chronicle.com/article/For-Study-Abroad-Offices /234306.

7. Kevin Kruse, *Stephen Covey: 10 Quotes That Can Change Your Life,* FORBES MAGAZINE, July 16, 2012.

8. Paula Koellmann, *Goss v. Lopez: How Much Process Is Really Due?*, 14 J. CONTEMP. LEGAL ISSUES 459, 465 (2004) (student disciplinary hearing conducted by phone conversation satisfied the due process hearing requirements). Sterrett v. Cowan, 85 F. Supp. 3d 916, 923 (E.D. Mich. 2015), *appeal dismissed* (Oct. 1, 2015) (factual allegations show that student parties or other witnesses may be interviewed remotely by audio or visual technology like Skype).

Chapter 4. Tactics

1. Edecio Martinez, *"Hofstra Rape Sex Tape": Student Saved from Criminal Charges,* CBS News, September 28, 2009, http://www.cbsnews.com /news/hofstra-rape-sex-tape-student-saved-from-criminal-charges/; Tobias Salinger, *Sigma Alpha Epsilon Closes University of Oklahoma Chapter Following Release of Racist Chant Video,* N.Y. DAILY NEWS, March 25, 2015, http://www.nydailynews.com/news/national/video -shows-sae-fraternity-members-university-oklaho-article-1.2142389.

2. Ronald S. Beitman, *Getting Your Hands on the Evidence: Heading to the Scene Be Ready, Be Safe, and Know What to Look For,* PRAC. LITIGATOR (May 2006), at 49 (in many cases investigators should be careful not to move physical evidence until it is first photographed in the position in which it was found); Scott A. Coffina, *Conducting Sound Internal Investigations: Now More Important Than Ever,* 21 CORP. GOV. ADV., no. 1 (January/February 2013), 11–16 (sound internal investigations are supported by early warning systems that allow for the collection of relevant documents and information that can give an organization the ability to respond proactively).

3. Cobb v. The Rector & Visitors of Univ. of Virginia, 69 F. Supp. 2d 815, 829 (W.D. Va. 1999) (courts have found that deviating from stated student disciplinary procedures does not constitute a violation of fundamental guarantees grounded in the due process clause); see also Jones v. Bd. of Governors of Univ. of North Carolina, 704 F.2d 713 (4th Cir.1983).

4. Fox v. Parker, 98 S.W.3d 713, 725 (Tex. App. 2003). In this case a faculty member claimed breach of obligation not to disclose information in a personnel file when student witnesses were informed of a pending investigation and termination proceeding regarding the faculty member. As a procedural matter, the court found that the University could inform student witnesses of a

pending investigation without breaching a confidentiality obligation with regard to information in a professor's personnel file.

5. Schaer v. Brandeis Univ., 432 Mass. 474, 478-79, 735 N.E.2d 373, 378 (2000).

6. As colleges and universities attempt to respond to sexual violence on campuses across the country, legislative enactments such as the Campus Sexual Violence Elimination Act (Campus SaVE Act), which was signed into law as part of the Violence Against Women Reauthorization Act of 2013 (VAWA) and which also amended the Clery Act, includes enhanced reporting requirements for sexual violence. Moreover, VAWA requires colleges and universities to report crimes of domestic violence, dating violence, stalking, and sexual assault. These statutes apply to public universities and private institutions participating in federal student financial aid programs.

7. James P. Timony, *Demeanor Credibility*, 49 CATHOLIC U. L. REV. 93 (2000); EEOC, *Enforcement Guidance: Vicarious Employer Liability for Unlawful Harassment by Supervisors*, No. 915002, June 18, 1999.

8. Policy guidance issued by the US Department of Education, Office of Civil Rights indicates that pursuant to Title IX individuals may be regarded as responsible employees of the school with an obligation to report incidents of sexual violence to appropriate authorities. A "responsible employee" has been defined as an individual with the authority to take action to prevent sexual violence, or one who has been given the duty of reporting incidents of sexual violence, or an employee who a student reasonably believes to have such authority or duty. See http://www2.ed.gov/about/offices/list/ocr/docs/qa -201404-title-ix.pdf; see also 34 C.F.R. § 106.8, 34 C.F.R. § 668.46. Under the Clery Act "campus security authorities" are required to report sexual assault and other crimes. These authorities include campus police and safety officers.

9. *Public Employee Could Be Fired for Refusing to Answer Questions About Alleged Unlawful Conduct*, 30 CAL. TORT REP. no. 3, 4 (March 2009) (a public employer may dismiss an employee for refusing to answer questions related to his job). Marvin F. Hill, Jr. & James A. Wright, *Employee Refusals to Cooperate in Internal Investigations: "Into the Woods" with Employers, Courts, and Labor Arbitrators*, 56 MO. L. REV., 869, 887-88 (1991) (a public employee's refusal to answer questions, after being directly ordered to do so and after being advised of

use-immunity, is a serious breach of duty that should not be tolerated by management).

10. Julianne M. Read, Martine B. Powell, Mark R. Kebbell, and Rebecca Milne. *Investigative Interviewing of Suspected Sex Offenders: A Review of What Constitutes Best Practice,* 11 INT. J. OF POLICE SCI & MAN., no. 4 (2009): 442–59.

11. Univ. of Texas Med. Sch. at Houston v. Than, 901 S.W.2d 926, 932 (Tex. 1995).

12. *Id.*

13. *Id.* The hearing officers were accompanied to the site where the test was conducted only by Dr. Margaret McNeese, an Associate Dean at the University of Texas at Houston. The accused student's request to participate in the test site visit was denied.

14. Dana O'Neil, *Ex-Ducks Dominic Artis and Damyean Dotson Suing School,* ESPN, Tuesday, March 15, 2016, http://espn.go.com/college-sports /story/_/id/14982683/two-former-oregon-ducks-file-lawsuit-dismissals (last viewed on March 16, 2016).

15. *Black's Law Dictionary* (9th ed., 2009).

16. *Ballentine's Law Dictionary* (3d ed., 1969).

17. However, students may be under certain obligations to cooperate with investigations authorized by policy. See Cottrell v. Nat'l Collegiate Athletic Ass'n, 975 So. 2d 306, 315 (Ala. 2007), which found that student-athletes and employees of institutions that are members of the NCAA are required by NCAA rules to cooperate fully with the investigation into and the resolution of the alleged rule violation. See also Anderson v. Vanderbilt Univ., No. 3-09-0095, 2010 WL 2196599, at *11 (M.D. Tenn. May 27, 2010), *aff'd,* 450 F. App'x 500 (6th Cir. 2011), which noted: "'the student-university relationship is contractual in nature although courts have rejected a rigid application of contract law in this area.' Doherty v. Southern College of Optometry, 862 F.2d 570, 577 (6th Cir.1988). Catalogs, manuals, handbooks, bulletins, circulars, and regulations of a university may help define this contractual relationship."

18. Coster v. DuQuette, 119 Conn. App. 827, 990 A.2d 362 (2010).

19. Charles Huckabee, *Harvard Reportedly Rescinds Admissions Offers to 10 Over Facebook Posts,* CHRON. HIGHER ED., June 4, 2017, http://www .chronicle.com/blogs/ticker/harvard-reportedly-rescinds-admissions -offers-to-10-over-facebook-posts/118797.

20. Ron Dicker, *Harvard Revokes Admissions from Students Who Shared Insensitive Memes*, HUFFINGTON POST, June 5, 2017, http://www.huffingtonpost.com/entry/harvard-revokes-admissions-for-students-who-posted-insensitive-memes_us_5935268ae4b075bff0f4db63.

21. American College of Trial Lawyers, *Recommended Practices for Companies and Their Counsel in Conducting Internal Investigations*, 46 AM. CRIM. L. REV. 73, 93 (2009).

22. Katherine Pankow, *Friend Request Denied: Chapter 619 Prohibits Colleges from Requesting Access to Social Media Accounts*, 44 MCGEORGE L. REV. 620, 623 (2013). This article discusses the prohibition on public and private colleges from requiring or requesting that students disclose their user names and passwords to their social media accounts, which can include an electronic service or account, or electronic content, including, but not limited to, videos or still photographs, blogs, video blogs, podcasts, instant and text messages, email, online services or accounts, or internet website profiles or locations.

23. Jack Stripling and Andy Thomason, *Was the University of Oklahoma President Too Quick to Condemn?*, NEWSWEEK, 3/12/15, http://www.newsweek.com/was-oklahoma-president-too-quick-condemn-313402. This article indicates that institutions are often in the difficult position of responding to hearsay, video evidence, media reports, or photographs.

24. Everett Starling, *Families Come Forward with Apologies for Roles in Racist OU Fraternity Video*, YAHOO NEWS, March 10, 2015, https://www.yahoo.com/news/families-come-forward-with-apologies-for-roles-in-racist-ou-fraternity-video-015233239.html?ref=gs).

25. Shari R. Veil and Rebekah A. Husted, *Best Practices as an Assessment for Crisis Communication*, J. COMM. MAN., 166, no. 2 (2012), 131–45.

26. Scott Weighart and Meghan McGrath, *How to Handle a Media Crisis.* MAN. HEALTHCARE EXEC. October 2015. Managed Healthcare Executive.com.

27. David Helfenbein, *Crisis Management 101: Taking Responsibility for Your Mistakes.* HUFFPOST POLITICS, Nov. 13, 2014. http://www.huffingtonpost.com/david-helfenbein/crisis-management-101-tak_b_6149276.html (last viewed April 20, 2016).

28. Lisa S. Kelsay, *Aftermath of a Crisis: How Colleges Respond to Prospective Students*, J. COLL. ADM. (Fall 2007), 197.

Chapter 5. Confidentiality and Privilege

1. A real-life incident at Baylor University in 2017 created quite a stir regarding the relationship between FERPA protections and the attorney-client privilege. Paul J. Gately, *BU: Jane Doe Plaintiffs' Request for Information Is Overbroad,* KWTX.COM (Woodway, TX), June 9, 2017, at http://www.kwtx.com/content/news/BU—Jane-Doe-plaintiffs -request-for-information-is-overbroad-427491413.html. See also Phillip Ericksen, *Baylor Ordered to Produce Long-Secretive Pepper Hamilton Information in Title IX Suit,* WACO TRIBUNE-HERALD, August 11, 2017, at http://www.wacotrib.com/news/courts_and_trials/baylor-ordered -to-produce-long-secretive-pepper-hamilton-information-in/article _e48e5d14-082e-5279-92f0-7fa73a5db207.html.

2. Frameworks for a lawsuit generally can be understood to have four distinctive components: (1) the pleading stage, which includes the complaint, answer, and amendment; (2) the discovery stage, which can be understood as the pretrial phase; (3) the trial, which can be held before a jury or only a judge; and (4) post-trial period, including the right for appeal.

3. Upjohn Co. v. United States, 449 U.S. 383, 389, 101 S. Ct. 677, 66 L. Ed.2d 584 (1981). The attorney-client privilege is the oldest of privileges for confidential information known to the common law. The privilege protects disclosure of communications but does not protect disclosure of the underlying facts.

4. Matthew Watkins, *Baylor Ordered to Turn Over Records from Sexual Assault Investigation,* TEXAS TRIBUNE, August 11, 2017, https://www .texastribune.org/2017/08/11/baylor-ordered-turn-over-documents -pepper-hamilton-report/.

5. Quagliarello v. Dewees, 802 F.Supp.2d 620, 632–33 (E.D. Pa. 2011). In this case attorney-client privilege was not waived when a student conferred with her lawyer in the presence of her parents because there was no intent to waive the privilege and the parents possessed a common interest with the student-client.

6. Sandra T.E. v. S. Berwyn Sch. Dist. 100, 600 F.3d 612, 620 (7th Cir. 2010). Note that the scope of legal services for which investigators are hired is important to the character of the legal advice sought by the institution.

7. Allan Ides and Christopher N. May, *Civil Procedure: Cases and Problems*, 2nd ed., New York: Aspen Publishers, 2006), 615.

8. The work-product rule established in *Hickman v. Taylor* eventually was codified in the Federal Rules of Civil Procedure, Fed.R.Civ.P. 26(b)(3).

9. *Duran v. Andrew*, No. 09-730 (HHK/AK), 2010 WL 1418344, at *4 (D.D.C. Apr. 5, 2010) (documents generated in the ordinary course of business irrespective of litigation are not protected by the work-product doctrine).

10. *Soter v. Cowles Pub. Co.*, 131 Wash. App. 882, 130 P.3d 840 (2006), aff'd, 162 Wash. 2d 716, 174 P.3d 60 (2007).

11. *Id.*

12. *Soter v. Cowles Pub. Co.*, 162 Wash. 2d 716, 174 P.3d 60 (2007).

13. Also referred to as the self-critical analysis privilege and the self-evaluative privilege.

14. Lawrence D. Finder and Maria Thompson Poirot, "Self-Critical Analyses and Internal Investigations: Ethical and Privilege Considerations for the Unwary," 13 ROCKY MOUNTAIN MINERAL LAW FOUNDATION INSTITUTE (April 2002); see also *Cooper Hospital/University Medical Center v. Sullivan*, 1998 WL 1297329, at *10 (D.N.J., 1998). "Those courts that recognize a federal self-critical analysis privilege generally require three criteria to be met for the information to qualify for protection: first, the information must result from critical self-analysis undertaken by the party seeking protection; second, the public must have a strong interest in preserving the free flow of the type of information sought; finally, the information must be of the type whose flow would be curtailed if discovery were allowed."

15. Eric Kelderman, *Education Dept. Warns of More Scrutiny for Accreditors*, CHRON. HIGHER ED., April 22, 2016, http://chronicle.com/blogs/ticker/education-dept-warns-of-more-scrutiny-for-accreditors/110644.

16. Oren R. Griffin, "Campus Safety, Policy, and Risk Management," in *Emerging Issues in College and University Campus Security: Leading Lawyers and Administrators on the Threats Confronting Our Campuses and the Laws That Protect Students, Staff, and Communities* (Thomson Reuters/Aspatore, 2015), 109–126.

17. James F. Flanagan, *Rejecting a General Privilege for Self-Critical Analysis*, 51 GEO. WASH. L. REV. 551, 574-76 (1983).
18. University of Kentucky v. Courier-Journal & Louisville Times Co., 830 S.W.2d at 376.
19. Highland Min. Co. v. West Virginia University School of Medicine, 235 W.Va. 370, 774 S.E.2d 36 (W.Va. 2015) (the burden of proof falls on the public body asserting the exemption to demonstrate that the public record should be protected from disclosure).
20. Lewis J. Heisman, J.D, *Power of Court under 5 U.S.C.A. § 552(a)(4)(b) to Examine Agency Records in Camera to Determine Propriety of Withholding Records,* 60 A.L.R. Fed. 416 (originally published in 1982). This article explores whether a FOIA exemption may be lawfully applied to the documents in question and whether the district court may examine the contents of the agency records in camera to determine the validity of the agency's decision to withhold the documents.
21. State Journal-Register v. University of Illinois Springfield, 994 N.E.2d at 714.
22. The Family Educational Rights and Privacy Act (FERPA), also known as the Buckley Amendment, is a federal law enacted to maintain the confidentiality of educational records for students in elementary and secondary schools as well as those in postsecondary institutions. The law carefully defines "educational records" and generally limits disclosure to students and their parents with some exceptions. See also chapter 2 for a discussion of FERPA and Kristin Knotts, *FOIA vs. FERPA/Scalia vs. Posner*, 38 S. ILL. U. L.J. 241 (2014).
23. See also Bauer v. Kincaid, 759 F. Supp. 575 (W.D. Mo. 1991); Chicago Tribune Co. v. Univ. of Illinois Bd. of Trustees, 781 F. Supp. 2d 672 (N.D. Ill. 2011), vacated sub nom, Chicago Tribune Co. v. Bd. of Trustees of Univ. of Illinois, 680 F.3d 1001 (7th Cir. 2012).
24. See State ex rel. The Miami Student v. Miami Univ., 79 Ohio St. 3d 168, 174, 680 N.E.2d 956, 961(Ohio 1997). (Dissenters in this Supreme Court of Ohio decision question the reliance on the Supreme Court of Georgia opinion: "The majority primarily relies on *Red & Black Publishing Co. v. Bd. of Regents of Univ. Sys. of Georgia* (1993), 262 Ga. 848, 427 S.E.2d 257, as authority for concluding that the disciplinary records in dispute are subject to release because they are not education records and, consequently, not subject to FERPA. However, *Red & Black* was decided prior to the 1995 amendments to

regulations implementing FERPA, in which the Secretary of Education clarified that disciplinary records were always included as education records under FERPA."); United States v. Miami Univ., 294 F.3d 797, 812 n.13 (6th Cir. 2002) (stating that some exemptions and exceptions, both in the statute and the DOE's regulations, have been added in response to prior case law).

25. Connoisseur Communication of Flint v. Univ. of Michigan, 230 Mich. App. 732, 584 N.W.2d 647 (1998) (acknowledging support for FERPA, here the plaintiffs' argument for disclosure was unpersuasive in light of state law that barred release of information under the Michigan Freedom of Information Act contrary to FERPA).

26. Chicago Tribune Co. v. Bd. of Trustees of Univ. of Ill., 680 F.3d 1001 (7th Cir. 2012). Here the court was confronted with a dispute that involved FERPA and the Illinois FOIA statute but based its decision on jurisdictional defects and not federal law. No federal agency decision was at issue and the matter did not depend on federal law but rather on a reading of state law—the Illinois Freedom of Information Act, 5 ILCS 140/1.

27. Press-Citizen Company Inc. vs. University of Iowa, 817 N.W.2d at 483-484.

28. *Id.* at 486-87.

29. *Id.* at 486.

30. Nick Estes, *State University Presidential Searches: Law and Practice*, 26 J.C. & U.L. 485 (2000).

31. Zbylski v. Douglas Cty. Sch. Dist., 154 F. Supp. 3d 1146 (D. Colo. 2015) (courts have found the duty to preserve to be triggered based on an internal investigation into an incident). See Marcum v. Scioto County, Ohio, No. 1:10-cv-790, 2013 WL 9557844, *7 (S.D. Ohio. Nov. 21, 2013).

32. The term "spoliation" has been defined as "[t]he intentional destruction, mutilation, alteration, or concealment of evidence, usually a document." *Black's Law Dictionary* (9th ed.).

33. Doe v. Norwalk Cmty. Coll., 248 F.R.D. 372, 377 (D. Conn. 2007).

34. Robert Friedman, "Understanding Counsel's Obligations and Challenges in the E-Discovery Process," in *The Role of Technology in Evidence Collection: Leading Lawyers on Preserving Electronic Evidence, Developing New Collection Strategies, and Understanding the Implications of Social Media* (Thomson Reuters/Aspatore, 2011), 61-74.

35. Minnesota E-Discovery Working Group 2, *Using Legal Holds for Electronic Discovery,* 40 WM. MITCHELL L. REV. 462, 471 (2014) (considering who is likely to possess documents and identifying potential custodians is an essential step in the legal hold process).

36. Michelle Casady, *Fired Baylor Athletics Employee Sues Pepper Hamilton,* December 14, 2016, https://www.law360.com/articles/872662/fired -baylor-athletics-employee-sues-pepper-hamilton.

37. Scott Jaschik, *Graham Spanier Sues Penn State and Louis Freeh,* INSIDE HIGHER ED, February 11, 2016, https://www.insidehighered.com /quicktakes/2016/02/11/graham-spanier-sues-penn-state-and-louis -freeh?width=775&height=500&iframe=true.

38. Harlow v. Fitzgerald, 457 U.S. 800, 818, 102 S. Ct. 2727, 73 L.Ed.2d 396 (1982) (leading US Supreme Court decision indicating that government officials are entitled to qualified immunity).

39. Tulsi Vembu v. The University of Massachusetts, and others (and a companion case) (2001 WL 35913225) (discussing the immunity defense, a Trial Order issued by a Superior Court of Massachusetts stated that state officials performing discretionary functions in their official capacity enjoy qualified immunity from civil suits for damages unless they acted with knowledge, or reason to know, that their conduct violated a person's clearly established constitutional rights). Also, for further discussion, see Pereira v. Commissioner of Social Services, 432 Mass. 251, 264–265 (2000) and Rodriques v. Furtado, 410 Mass. 878, 882 (1991).

40. De Jong v. Metro. State Univ., No. A12-0829, 2012 WL 5990306, at *2 (Minn. Ct. App. Dec. 3, 2012).

Chapter 6. Results and Outcomes

1. See also Sara Lipka, *Judge Rules for Expelled Student Who Sued a Fellow Student Over Plagiarism,* CHRON. HIGHER ED., December 5, 2008, http://www.chronicle.com/article/Judge-Rules-for-Expelled/1389.

2. In the United States District Court for the Western District of Missouri En Banc, 45 F.R.D. 133, 145 (1969) (noting with respect to institutions of higher education, "[i]n the field of discipline, scholastic and behavioral, an institution may establish any standards reasonably relevant to the lawful missions, processes, and functions of the institution").

3. Ellen L. Mossman, *Navigating a Legal Dilemma: A Student's Right to Legal Counsel in Disciplinary Hearings for Criminal Misbehavior,* 160 U. PA. L. REV. 585 (2012).

4. Gabrilowitz v. Newman, 582 F.2d 100 (1st Cir. 1978) (noting that a student may be entitled to legal counsel where the student may face criminal charges relative to issues raised in a campus disciplinary hearing).

5. *French,* 303 F. Supp. at 1337. It is worth noting that the district court pointed out that the US Court of Appeals for the Second Circuit had rejected the student's right to be represented by counsel in disciplinary proceedings, citing Madera v. Board of Education of City of New York, 386 F.2d 778 (2nd Cir. 1967) and Wasson v. Trowbridge, 382 F.2d 807 (2nd Cir. 1967). The court also cited other district court decisions that allowed the students to be represented by legal counsel and secondary sources examining the issue: Zanders v. Louisiana State Board of Education, 281 F.Supp. 747, 752 (E.D. La. 1968); Esteban v. Central Missouri State College, 277 F.Supp. 649, 651 (W.D. Mo. 1968). See Charles Alan Wright, *The Constitution on the Campus,* 22 VAND L.REV. 1027, 1075 (1969), which supports the right to counsel for students undergoing major disciplinary proceedings at colleges and universities. See also Arthur Sherry, *Governance of the University: Rules, Rights, and Responsibilities,* 54 CALIF. L. REV. 23, 37 (1966), which also supports a student's right to counsel in a university disciplinary proceeding that is of sufficient gravity.

6. Flaim v. Medical College of Ohio, 418 F.3d 629, 640 (6th Cir. 2005); *French,* 303 F. Supp. at 1337. See also Douglas R. Richmond, *Students' Right to Counsel in University Disciplinary Proceedings,* 15 J.C. & U.L. 289, 299 (1989).

7. Curtis J. Berger and Vivian Berger, *Academic Discipline: A Guide to Fair Process for the University Student,* 99 COLUM. L. REV. 289, 343 (1999).

8. *Procedural Due Process for School Discipline: Probing the Constitutional Outline,* 119 U. PA. L. REV. 545, 610 (1971) (a lawyer can assist a student in making well-considered statements).

9. A. Calhoun, *Introducing Restorative Justice: Re-visioning Responses to Wrongdoing,* PREVENTION RESEARCHER, 20(1) (2013), 4–8.

10. Boyd v. State Univ. of New York at Cortland, 110 A.D.3d 1174, 1176, 973 N.Y.S.2d 413, 415–416 (2013). The court noted that the University's

reliance on the testimony of a University of Delaware police officer at the disciplinary hearing was not helpful because the officer's explanation of the Delaware crimes involved was not consistent with the Delaware Criminal Code.

11. *Id.,* at 1175.

12. J. J. Sloan, *The Modern Campus Police: An Analysis of Their Evolution, Structure, and Function,* AM. J. POLICE, 11, no.1 (1992), 85-104 (discusses the development of campus police departments in institutions of higher education). See also J. C. Wada, R. Patten, and K. Candela, *Betwixt and Between: The Perceived Legitimacy of Campus Police,* POLICING: INT. J. POLICE STRAT. & MAN. 33, no. 1 (2010), 114-31.

13. National Center for Education Statistics, *120 Years of American Education: A Statistical Portrait,* http://nces.ed.gov/pubs93/93442.pdf (last viewed July 24, 2016). The 1950s and 1960s marked two major developments. First, large numbers of young people entered college and second, public colleges expanded dramatically to meet the demand. College enrollment rose by 49 percent in the 1950s, partly because of the rise in the enrollment/population ratio from 15 percent to 24 percent. During the 1960s, enrollment rose by 120 percent. By 1969, college enrollment was as large as 35 percent of the 18- to 24-year-old population. About 41 percent of the college students were women. Public institutions accounted for 74 percent of enrollment, and about one-fourth of all students were enrolled at 2-year colleges.

14. Jan Walbert et al., *In Search of Safer Communities: Emerging Practices for Student Affairs in Addressing Campus Violence,* NEW DIRECTIONS FOR STUDENT SERVICES (Winter 2008), Supplement, 1-38; Janelle Penny. *Crisis Averted?* BUILDINGS 105, no. 9 (September 2011), 50-54.

15. Mark K. Neville, Jr. *The Foreign Corrupt Practices Act: Conducting Internal Investigations* ¶ 19.06 in INTERNATIONAL TRADE LAWS OF THE UNITED STATES (Thomson Reuters, 2018).

16. Daniel J. Fetterman and Mark P. Goodman, eds., *Defending Corporations and Individuals in Government Investigations* (Thomson West, 2012), § 3:36, "Reporting the Results of the Internal Investigation."

17. Lauren Bragin, *Is Live Trial Testimony Permissible? A Primer on Rule 30(b)(6) Witnesses,* 57 DRI FOR THE DEFENSE, no. 4 (April 2015), 26-29, http://www.glaserweil.com/uploads/Lauren_Bragin_-_A_Primer_on

_Rule_30(b)(6)_Witnesses_Bragin_2015.pdf. Note that the testimony may be excluded where a witness lacks personal knowledge. See *Union Pump Co. v. Centrifugal Tech. Inc.*, 404 F. App'x 899, 908 (5th Cir. 2010), wherein the testimony of a witness was excluded regarding a series of internal investigations when no written reports were issued as a result of the investigations because the witness did not conduct or have any role in the internal investigation but learned of the facts through conversations with others.

18. Kenneth Winer, *International Investigations in a Global Economy: Preparing a Report of the Investigation,* 2 LAWS OF INTERNATIONAL TRADE, § 45:7 (Thomson Reuters, August 2017).

Conclusion

1. Thomas J. Hernandez and Deborah L. Fister, *Dealing with Disruptive and Emotional College Students: A Systems Model,* 4 J. COLL. COUN. (Spring 2001), 49-62.

2. Beth M. Schwartz, Holly E. Tatum, and Megan C. Hageman, *College Students' Perception of and Responses to Cheating at Traditional, Modified, and Non-Honor System Institutions,* ETHICS & BEHAV., 23(6) (2013), 463-76.

3. Thomas R. Baker, *Judicial Complaint Resolution Models for Higher Education: An Administrator's Reference Guide* (Horsham, PA: LRP Publications, 2005).

4. *Id.* at 24.

5. Sarah M. Marshall, Megan Moore Gardner, Carole Hughes, and Ute Lowery, *Attrition from Student Affairs: Perspectives from Those Who Exited the Profession,* 53 J. STUDENT AFF. RES. & PRAC. (2016), 2, 146-59.

Index

collusion, witness, 122

communication: crisis plan, 124-26; and encouraging students to come forward, 61, 101, 109; and facilitating dialogue, 156; with media, 101-2, 106, 124-26; modes of, 97; and privilege, 144-47; reporting chain, 96-98; of reports, 160-63. *See also* documents and electronic information

compelled testimony, 57-58

complaint in litigation, 16-17, 190n2

complexity. *See* scope and complexity of investigations

compliance, 13-19, 32-33, 34, 44, 162

confidentiality and privilege: attorney-client privilege, 87, 98, 100, 129-32; breach of employee's, 186n4; case study, 127-28; and charge of investigation, 87; and ex parte actions, 116-18; and FOIA, 138-42; inability to guarantee, 179n54; and managing communication, 144-47; and media, 102; overview, 128-29; and preserving documents, 123, 142-44, 160; and qualified privilege, 146-47; and reporting chain, 97-98; and reports, 131, 163; and self-critical evaluation privilege, 136-38; and work-product doctrine, 87, 100, 132-35

conflict checks, 73

constitutional considerations: and aspirations, 3-6, 25-30; case study, 23-24; Fifth Amendment, 54-58; First Amendment, 36, 38-49; Fourteenth Amendment, 50, 58-62; Fourth Amendment, 49-54; institution's role in, 24-25; overview, 24-25; and right to counsel, 151-54; and right to

interview or question, 45-47; and state action doctrine, 35-38, 42-43, 54. *See also* due process

corrective actions, 7, 165. *See also* disciplinary action; prevention

counsel, right to, 151-54

credibility: and assessing witnesses, 106, 111-13, 120-21, 122; of investigators, 89-90; and personal knowledge, 119; and reporting chain, 98

Crime Awareness and Campus Security Act of 1990. *See* Clery Act

crime statistics, 8, 65, 70-71, 187n6, 187n8

criminal activity: and criminal investigations and prosecutions, 46-47, 107-8; and Fifth Amendment, 55-56, 57-58; as justification for investigation, 31, 34; and right to counsel, 151-54

custodial responsibilities, 146-47

custody, 108, 123, 144, 160

"Dear Colleague Letters," ix, 72-73, 182n21

decision-making in trajectory, 12, 13

defamation, 39, 146, 163

demeanor, and evaluating witness, 111-12

Department of Education (DOE), 72-73, 76, 136, 140, 183n22

Department of Education's Office for Civil Rights. *See* OCR

designated public forum, 42-43

disciplinary action: and careful and deliberate standards, 59-62; and design of disciplinary systems, 165-70; and disclosure of records, 139-40, 192n24; and institutional mission, 150-51, 164-65, 167, 168; vs. restorative